THE VEGAN COMFORT KITCHEN

Simple, Delicious and Deeply Satisfying Plant-Based Recipes

DEB GLEASON

FOREWORD BY GENE BAUR

Any omission, paraphrasing, or misattribution is unintentional. If you find an error, please forward documentation to the author for the next edition.

Published by: Deb Gleason Publishing, debgleason.net
Food photography: Deb Gleason
Cover and interior design: Deb Ozarko, debozarko.com
Printed by: CreateSpace, an Amazon.com company

ISBN: 978-0-9949845-3-1

Available from Amazon.com and other online stores.

THIS BOOK IS DEDICATED TO NIKKI AND THE TRILLIONS OF PIGS, COWS, CHICKENS, TURKEYS, GOATS, FISH, AND SEA CREATURES WHO ARE PREDATED UPON EVERY YEAR BY HUMANITY FOR NOTHING MORE THAN A FICTITIOUS, YET WIDELY ACCEPTED BELIEF SYSTEM THAT IMPLIES THAT THE CONSUMPTION OF FLESH, DAIRY AND EGGS IS NECESSARY FOR HEALTH AND WELL-BEING.

TOGETHER MAY WE AWAKEN FROM THE SPELL OF CULTURAL CONDITIONING AND OPEN OUR HEARTS AND MINDS TO THE ABUNDANCE, JOY AND NATURAL VITALITY OF PLANT-BASED LIVING.

MAY YOU ENJOY THE PHYSICAL, EMOTIONAL AND SPIRITUAL WELL-BEING THAT COMES WITH ANIMALS IN YOUR HEART AND PLANTS IN YOUR BELLY.

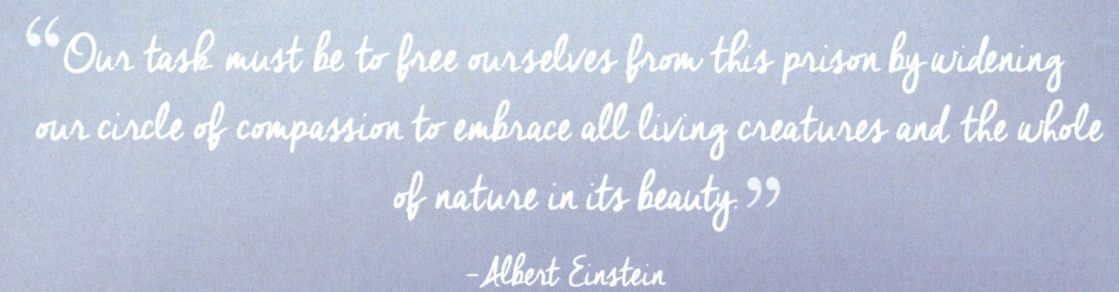
"Our task must be to free ourselves from this prison by widening our circle of compassion to embrace all living creatures and the whole of nature in its beauty."
-Albert Einstein

CONTENTS

FOREWORD
BY GENE BAUR

I am grateful for Deb and her voice of conscience, and I love how she makes vegan living so easy and understandable in *The Vegan Comfort Kitchen*. She also makes it fun and tasty with her amazing recipes. Eating plants instead of animals is good for people, other animals, and the planet.

It has been estimated that we could save trillions of dollars on health care costs by shifting to eating a whole foods plant based diet, instead of eating artery clogging animal products. Hundreds of millions of citizens around the globe suffer from chronic illnesses, like heart disease, which could be prevented or reversed by eating plants instead of animal products. We can turn our health around, get off of medication, and improve our lives by changing how we eat.

Plant based agriculture is so much more sensible and efficient than animal agriculture. Growing and harvesting corn, soybeans and other crops to feed farm animals and fatten them for slaughter requires vast quantities of land, water, fossil fuel, and other resources. We could feed ten times more people through plant based agriculture rather than animal agriculture. Tragically, as the human population has increased, rainforests and other natural ecosystems have been wiped out and turned into cropland or pasture to grow feed crops or to graze animals in order to meet the escalating demand for meat. The United Nations warns that we need to curtail our consumption of animal foods because animal agriculture is among the top contributors to our planet's most significant environmental threats, including climate change and the loss of biodiversity. We are now living in what scientists call the anthropocene epoch, a geological era defined by the significant, planet altering impacts of human activity, and the exploitation of animals for meat, milk and eggs is a major contributor.

Every year, billions of animals—trillions when you include fish—are killed to satisfy our desire for meat, milk and eggs. Most of us living in developed countries become accustomed to eating animal foods, without thinking about the cows, pigs, chickens, fishes, and other animals who suffered and died in the process. We are led to believe that eating animal foods provides us with essential nutrients for optimal health and well-being. In fact, eating animal foods like we do is hazardous.

"Choosing to eat plants instead of animals benefits our health, and allows us to live more compassionately on Earth."

Choosing to eat plants instead of animals benefits our health, and allows us to live more compassionately on Earth. Killing animals for food is violent and desensitizing. It requires that we shut down our empathy and lose part of our humanity. It is bad for animals, and it is also bad for us. Can you imagine what it would be like to work in a slaughterhouse? Such work obliges us to close our eyes and numb our hearts to the fact that we are killing living, feeling individuals.

Like all animals, farm animals have complex cognitive and emotional lives, each experiencing this world in his, or her, own way. They remember past events, develop personal relationships with other animals and people, and they have likes and dislikes. Like all of us, they want to be treated with compassion and respect. At Farm Sanctuary, we see farm animals as friends, not food. We rescue and care for survivors of the factory farm industry, and nurse them back to health. The animals arrive with painful memories of the past, having only known cruelty at human hands. But once they feel safe and come to understand human kindness, their fear subsides. They recover physically and psychologically, and they begin to flourish and enjoy life. Eventually, they even seek out human companionship. We have turkeys, for example, who love people. They follow you around like puppy dogs, and will sit on your lap when given the chance.

Our lives are enriched when human and nonhuman animals engage in life affirming, mutually beneficial relationships. Kindness to animals benefits humanity in so many ways, including when that kindness moves us to eat with conscience. How we eat has a profound impact on ourselves and our planet, and we can each make a positive difference through conscientious food choices that are aligned with our values and interests. Small daily actions add up, and cumulatively, can create a better world, and this book can help.

Gene Baur,
Co-founder and President of Farm Sanctuary

INTRODUCTION
EAT FROM LOVE, LOVE WHAT YOU EAT

A friend of mine once said, "I don't want to participate in things that break my heart." This is exactly what prompted my own vegan journey in the year 2000. The horrifying reality of the animal agriculture system broke my heart, and it was clear to me that I could no longer participate in this madness.

My first career out of university was in policing. It wasn't exactly what I had in mind when I commenced my studies, but it turned out to be a perfect fit for who I was back then. I fast-tracked my way from uniformed constable to homicide detective in four short years.

I was a tenacious homicide detective, eager to bring justice to traumatized families. My daily toolkit included: lie detector tests, massive and complex undercover operations, wire taps, stake outs, search warrants, spin teams, and gruelling interrogations. I used these tools to organize information, outsmart bad guys, dig deep into the story, and discover the truth.

Those years flew by in a sleep-deprived, pager-weary blur, and during that time I got an insider's view into the resources—both human and monetary—that are poured into piecing together a crime that has taken a human life.

I had promised myself early on in this career that I would hang up my gun and badge if I could sense I was becoming as cold, distant and shut down as some of the more seasoned detectives around me appeared to be.

In the year 2000, I kept my promise. At the age of 29, I left behind a flourishing career where my potential seemed limitless, but I was feeling caged. As my policing career was ending, something amazing happened—in fact it was so amazing, that it became the start of another completely unpredictable journey.

Allow me to set the stage.

At this time in my life, I was eating exactly as culture had trained me: heavy on meat, dairy, processed and fast foods. I was essentially eating what my parents, friends, and co-workers were eating without thinking about the consequences. The consequences included having my gallbladder removed when I was in my early 20's. I had no clue back then that this was connected to my dietary choices, and so I carried on with my unconscious, habitual, and familiar way of living and eating.

One evening after a long policing shift (shortly before my departure from the force), I rented an innocent-looking documentary called Baraka. It included a small clip from an egg-laying facility that stunned me. I watched newborn chicks travelling down a fast conveyor belt as they were examined and sorted by factory workers. Some were returned to the conveyor belt where they continued along to their destination, and some were dropped into a big swirling metal tube. I was profoundly disturbed by this scene. Something penetrated the depths of my heart. I knew what I was seeing was terribly wrong.

I called Deb Ozarko—who was only the second vegan I'd ever met, and my soon-to-be life partner—and described to her what I had seen. I asked her what those baby chicks were doing in a factory, and what happened to the ones that went down the metal tube. Before she answered, she asked me a life-altering question that I will never forget. She asked, "Do you really want to know?" I mustered up the courage to say "Yes". The answer changed me, forever.

The truth about factory farming practices immediately sank in. Understanding how broken our food system is, turned me vegetarian overnight and led me down a path to veganism a month later.

It was a hard month, a month of shock, anger, rage, and grief as I learned the dark truth about animal agriculture. As I digested the reality of where my meat, dairy and eggs had been coming from, I made a commitment to never again participate in the exploitation of animals to suit my taste buds or my cultural conditioning.

Up until that time I had been focused on homicides, but I quickly realized that there were much bigger killers all around me. Our meat and dairy-centric food choices were killing trillions of animals every year, and creating fatal disease in about half the people in North America in the form of heart disease. On top of all of this, animal agriculture was killing the planet with global warming emissions that surpassed even those of the entire transportation industry. I was waking up to an inconvenient, yet empowering truth.

Shortly after my departure from the police force, I went back to school to become a Holistic Nutritionist. I began honing my cooking and recipe design skills so I could empower others who were interested in a plant-powered lifestyle.

While one chapter was closing in my life, a more expansive one was opening. The passion I had for bringing criminals to justice was replaced with a passion to bring light to an unjust and harmful system that was killing people, the planet and the animals we share it with. I traded in search warrants and lie detectors tests for vegan cooking demos, classes, courses, and coaching.

My own wake-up call was an invitation to honor my deep intuition and to trust myself when it came to my own ability to properly, and compassionately nourish myself. It has been a profound honor to empower others to do the same.

When I chose to eat from the animal world many years ago, I was not as vibrant, activated and alive as I am now. Being vegan continually expands the space to be a peaceful part of this magical, earthly experience.

For the last decade, my passion in this world has been to shift food culture toward a healthy, delicious and abundant vegan lifestyle.

Living a life that is whole, clean and powerful begins in your own kitchen. This cookbook is filled with the same meals, snacks, desserts, and other delicious fare made regularly in my own kitchen. It also brings together the very best of the recipes I've created in my 17 years of experimenting with amazing plant-based ingredients including the best of my vegan cooking classes, and my vegan television cooking show.

If you are interested in making delicious, healthy, and comforting vegan food at home, this book is for you. The recipes are simple and do not require fancy or hard-to-find ingredients. Using whole plant ingredients, the meals are fast and easy to prepare, so you can get in and out of the kitchen in record time.

This book is perfect for a single person, couples, and entire families, including ideas on how to fuel big and little bodies to the maximum as you enjoy every delicious, healthy mouthful of food.

Here's to animals in your heart, and plants in your belly.

RESCUING NIKKI AND FRIENDS

One of the amazing jobs that followed my policing career was as an animal rescue technician with IFAW (International Fund for Animal Welfare). It was a challenging and rewarding career that was a natural fit for the emergency responder in me. I received extensive training in swift water rescue, wilderness survival, emergency management, and so much more. I was on a team of highly trained rescue technicians that responded to disasters around the world with the fulfilling task of saving animals.

One of the standout rescue experiences that influences me to this day, happened in Iowa in June of 2008. After several days of intense rain, the Iowa River near the mouth of the Mississippi flooded. When the floodwaters became too great to contain, the levee burst and suddenly the largest pork producing area in the United States was underwater. The situation was dire. The flooding was so extensive that the sea of farms and cornfields peppering the landscape were no longer visible. All that remained to be seen through the murky waters were rooftops and hydro poles.

While several thousand pigs were rushed to slaughter—the farmers' solution to impending economic loss—many farmers decided to simply abandon their pigs to fend for themselves. Thousands of pigs drowned, either while still trapped in their intensive confinement facilities, or after being swept out of these sheds by rapid currents.

By nature, pigs are good swimmers. Some of the pigs in this disaster were strong enough to swim to the shore of the levee and drag themselves out of the water. When the townspeople spotted the pigs who were fortunate enough to make it to the levee, the Sheriff's Department was called in to destroy them. Images of the surviving pigs being shot and killed were aired on CNN. The brutality did not sit well with viewers however, and a significant public backlash followed. IFAW, together with Farm Sanctuary, American Humane and the Animal Rescue League of Boston were called into action to rescue the remaining pigs.

When we arrived in Iowa, we were aware of the surviving pigs on the levee. We knew they were most likely suffering from dehydration, starvation and burns from sun exposure. These pigs would have never known anything outside of their confinement sheds, and they were now exposed to brutal sun and heat. The water on both sides of the levee was also highly contaminated from the flooding, and they would have to rely on their instincts to find what little wild food was available to eat.

On the first day of the rescue we headed out in small boats filled with pig feed, sunscreen and electrolyte fluids. As we approached the levee my stomach lurched. For as far as the eye could see, there was nothing but death. Hundreds of dead pigs lined the shore of the levee. The sight and the stench were excruciating. We walked the levee for hours, stepping over an endless sea of dead pigs, in search for the few pigs we hoped to find alive. It seemed hopeless. After many desperate hours, we found one, then two, then three living pigs. What an amazing feeling to know we were not too late!

As suspected, the animals were in rough shape. Transporting them by boat was too risky, and it was a 20-mile-walk back to town at the other end of the levee. If we were able to get them that far, it would be easy to load them onto a trailer and bring them to safety. While the levee was strong, stable and about 25 feet wide, we did not have legal permission to drive a tractor and trailer onto it. Our plan was to return each day and slowly walk the surviving pigs along the levee back to town.

Day after day, we went out to the levee to drop off food and provide them with large pails of electrolyte fluids. Every day, we found more living pigs. All were in rough shape, clearly malnourished and badly sunburned. We set up tents for shade, and when they seemed strong enough, we continued walking them as a group toward the end of the levee.

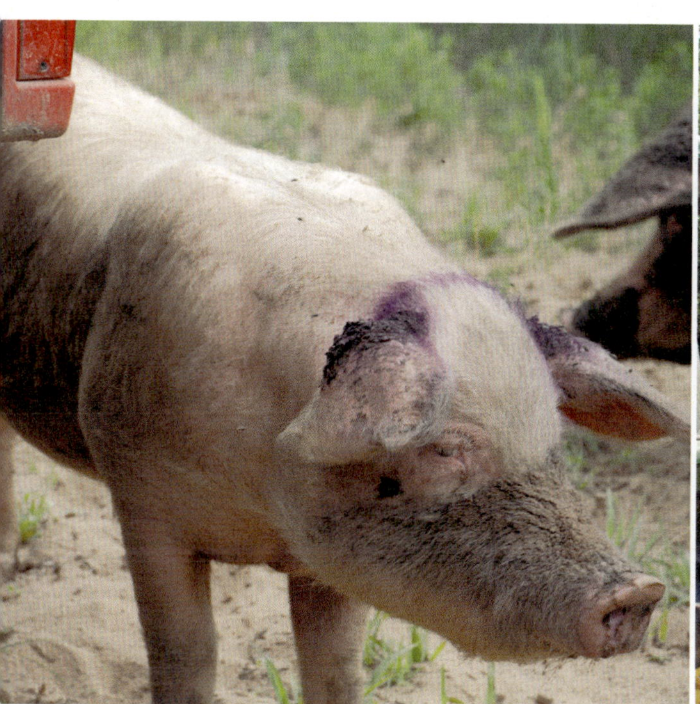

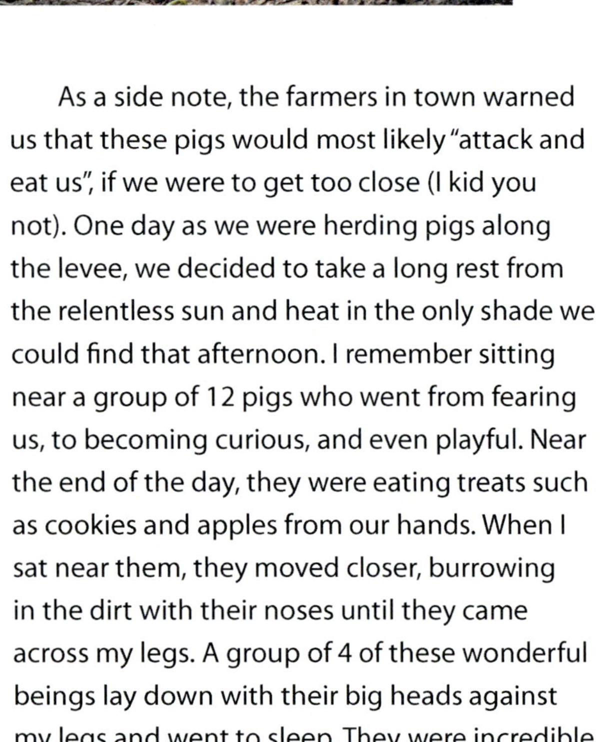

As a side note, the farmers in town warned us that these pigs would most likely "attack and eat us", if we were to get too close (I kid you not). One day as we were herding pigs along the levee, we decided to take a long rest from the relentless sun and heat in the only shade we could find that afternoon. I remember sitting near a group of 12 pigs who went from fearing us, to becoming curious, and even playful. Near the end of the day, they were eating treats such as cookies and apples from our hands. When I sat near them, they moved closer, burrowing in the dirt with their noses until they came across my legs. A group of 4 of these wonderful beings lay down with their big heads against my legs and went to sleep. They were incredible animals who displayed both emotion and intelligence, even under these harsh conditions. It was deeply moving to witness the evolution of a trust in humans for the first time in their brutalized lives. We were in this together, battling the sun, the incessantly-biting gnats and the culture all around us that said this was impossible and trivial. To the locals, the economics did not make sense because we were putting in more time and effort than the pigs had value. We did not agree.

With the hard work of Farm Sanctuary's Julie Janovsky, we finally got approval to bring a tractor and trailer onto the levee about a week into the rescue. It felt like a miracle. Instead of slowly walking the pigs for 20 miles to the end of the levee, we could quickly transport them to safety in a matter of days. We borrowed a hydraulic trailer from a farmer in the area who had not been impacted by the flooding. Together with Farm Santuary's, Chuck Pappas and Dan D'Eramo, I went to pick up the trailer at his farm, and while waiting for him to bring the trailer, I walked over to a confinement building expecting it to be empty. As I peered over the cement wall, I was haunted by a horrifying image: hundreds of female pigs, laying on their sides on a concrete floor, immobilized by the metal bars of gestation crates. Gestation crates are metal enclosures that intensely confine female breeding pigs during pregnancy, which sadly is most of their adult lives.

Breeding sows are first impregnated when they are only seven months old. They endure two to three pregnancies per year, before their bodies become so worn out that they are slaughtered—all before they reach the tender age of three.

The cages I saw were so tight, and the conditions so cramped, that the pigs could not stand up or move around. My eyes focused in on one pig who had her head on the ground. She was breathing, but her life force was absent. Tears streamed down my cheeks, as the word "languishing" swirled through my mind. She was so pink and perfect, and I knew she would never get a chance to feel a belly rub or a mud bath; she would never know love, peace or trust. She was just an economic commodity—a producer of piglets—all of whom would eventually become cheap bacon.

It was a surreal moment. While I was feeling emotionally crushed about what I'd just seen, I was also feeling gratitude for use of the trailer so we could get the rest of the pigs off the levee and into safety.

Driving a tractor and trailer onto the levee changed everything. Within a couple of days we had safely transported all the pigs from the levee. Each night as we brought yet another group of pigs to the holding barn—which ironically was an abandoned stockyard—we would spend time hanging out with them, feeding them, treating their sunburns and offering water, which they would drink out of massive jugs by hand. They were in the incredible care of Susie Coston, Farm Sanctuary's National Shelter Director. Susie lovingly and skillfully nursed them back to health so they were well prepared for the long drive home to Farm Sanctuary, the largest and most effective farm animal rescue and protection organization in the United States.

While my days were full of both agony and elation, there was one day in particular that stands out as very special. At the end of the levee closer to town, another live pig was spotted laying in the brush. Upon closer inspection, we found a mother and her seven newborn piglets. This amazing girl, who was later named Nikki, had swum to safety with a full-term pregnancy and given birth to her litter after the flood. Despite her own comprised health, she had built her seven new babies a nest in the thick brush and was feeding them and keeping them safe.

The piglets were the cutest things, like little pink puppies. We observed Nikki leaving the nest several times to check us out. Her seven little ones would initially be hot on her heels, and would just as quickly run back to the safety of the nest. We knew she would probably never leave her babies to come with us, so our plan was to put a snow fence around the nest the next time she left it to keep the babies in one place as we walked Nikki to the awaiting trailer. To do this we created a walking pen, which

was essentially four large metal fence panels with two people holding the ends of each one. The next time Nikki ventured away from the nest, we closed her into the moving pen. Eight humans and one pig slowly walked towards the trailer where she walked up the ramp with ease.

Working with the local vet, we carefully picked up each of the seven piglets, placed them in a dog carrier and delivered them to Nikki who was eagerly waiting in the trailer. When we got the family to the holding facility, the piglets were happy to resume nursing, as Nikki finally got some proper nourishment and hydration. Participating in Nikki's amazing rescue remains a highlight of my life to this date.

After almost two weeks of rescuing pigs, we concluded our efforts. Sixty-nine pigs were saved. All of the rescued pigs were transported to Farm Sanctuary in upstate New York to begin a new lease on life. From an abandoned commodity left to drown, to a respected sentient being who would be loved and cared for the remainder of their natural lives. This was truly a happy ending!

Nikki lived for another eight years at Farm Sanctuary under Susie's loving care. She was a funny, talkative and beautiful being, who was an incredibly loving mother. Nikki made a nest for her babies every night, even after they grew to be bigger than she was.

I visited Nikki a couple of times after the rescue, and she always remembered me. It was breathtaking to have her run to me when I arrived, tears of joy streaming down my face and beautiful sounds of joy streaming from her.

Nikki battled illness for most of her years at Farm Sanctuary. When she arrived, she had antibiotic-resistant abscesses on her neck. She developed arthritis and other afflictions over the years, most likely due to being intensively confined and raised on concrete. She had multiple, long hospital stays and returned home to the Farm each time to her excited adult kids. In 2016, after eight years of knowing the sweet taste of pure love, she left this world.

This book is dedicated to Nikki and the trillions of animals like her whose voices are unheard in our world.

Columbia

VEGAN KITCHEN PANTRY

While you don't need to rush out and buy everything at once, having many of these items on-hand will help you get right into the kitchen and immediately whip up the delicious recipes in this book. I recommend that you use this list as a guide as you grow and maintain your vegan pantry. What I haven't listed are the fresh fruits , vegetables and herbs you will need for specific meals. Having a wide variety on hand will make things easier and will also make your dining experiences nutritious and delicious.

DRIED HERBS

Basil
Dill
Poultry seasoning (a mix of sage, rosemary, thyme)
Sage
Rosemary
Onion powder
Garlic powder
Cumin
Chili powder

GRAINS & FLOURS

Quinoa
Brown rice
Brown rice flour
Rolled oats
Spelt flour
Cornmeal
Wild rice
Millet

LEGUMES AND LEGUME PRODUCTS

Miso
Soy milk
Low-sodium soy sauce
Tamari
Tofu: firm or extra firm
Soft or silken tofu
Red lentils
Brown (green) lentils
Chickpeas (canned or dry)
Black beans (canned or dry)

BETTER THAN DAIRY

Dairy-free cheese shreds
Egg-free mayonnaise
Plant-based milks (soy, rice, cashew, almond etc.)
Soy or coconut yogurt
Dairy free ice cream (soy, coconut, almond, cashew, etc.)

SPICES, SEASONINGS AND CONDIMENTS

Ground and fresh ginger
Ground and fresh turmeric
Sea salt
Pepper
Nutritional yeast
Sun dried tomatoes
Pure vanilla extract

THINGS IN CANS AND JARS

Tomato paste
Tomato sauce
Canned whole tomatoes
Canned chopped tomatoes
Black olives
Green olives
Vegetable broth
Coconut milk (full fat)
Salsa
Artichokes
Unsweetened applesauce

OILS & VINEGARS

Coconut oil
Vegetable oil (safflower, sunflower)
Extra virgin olive oil
Toasted sesame oil
Apple cider vinegar
Balsamic vinegar
Seasoned rice vinegar

PASTA & NOODLES

Rice noodles
Lasagna noodles
Spaghetti noodles
Soba noodles

BREADY THINGS

Whole grain pizza shells
Whole grain flour tortillas or rice tortillas

NUTS & SEEDS

Almond butter
Peanut butter
Flax seeds
Chia seeds
Tahini
Hemp seeds (hearts)
Walnuts
Almonds
Cashews
Pumpkin seeds
Sesame seeds

SWEETENERS, DRIED FRUIT AND CHOCOLATE

Semi-sweet or dark chocolate chips (dairy-free)
Maple syrup
Unrefined sugar (e.g. Sucanat, coconut sugar, evaporated cane juice)
Dried cranberries
Raisins
Cocoa powder
Cacao powder (raw, unprocessed cocoa)
Cacao nibs
Unsweetened shredded coconut
Big soft dates (e.g. Medjool)

Neapolitan Shake (page 32)

Chapter 1

DRINKS

VANILLA CASHEW MILK

This is my favorite milk for tea, cereal and baking. I keep some in the fridge at all times and never tire of its creaminess. You can adjust the quantity of water to suit your taste. More water will mean a thinner milk, and less will make it thicker and creamier. One of the best parts about this milk is that, unlike almond milk, it does not need to be strained. Just blend and drink.

MAKES 7 CUPS

6 cups water

1 cup raw cashews

2 pitted dates

1 teaspoon pure vanilla extract

Soak cashews for a minimum of four hours by covering them with water in a bowl. Drain and rinse.

Place all ingredients in a blender and blend for one minute or until smooth. Pour into a container and store in the fridge for up to five days.

CHOCOLATE TOASTED HAZELNUT MILK

This milk tastes like Ferrero Rocher chocolates melted in a glass. Drink on its own, or try it in coffee for a truly awesome experience.

MAKES 4 CUPS

3 cups water

1 cup raw hazelnuts (filberts)

4 pitted dates or ¼ cup maple syrup

3 tablespoons raw cacao powder or cocoa powder

1 teaspoon pure vanilla extract

Pinch of sea salt

Heat oven to 325°F and toast hazelnuts on a cookie sheet for 10-12 minutes or until fragrant. Keep a close eye on them so they don't burn, and stir at least once while baking. Allow the hazelnuts to cool.

Add the toasted hazelnuts and remaining ingredients in a blender and blend for one minute or until smooth.

Pour and enjoy.

FRENCH VANILLA CASHEW CREAMER

Sweet and thick, this creamer will take your coffee to the next level of comfort.

MAKES 1.5 CUPS

- **1 cup water**
- **½ cup raw cashews, soaked**
- **2 pitted dates**
- **1 teaspoon pure vanilla extract**

Soak cashews in water for a minimum of four hours. Drain and rinse. Place ingredients in a blender and blend for one minute or until smooth. Pour into a container, and store in the fridge for up to five days.

CHOCOLATE PEANUT BUTTER SHAKE

I am always in search of the perfect chocolate and peanut butter combination and I found it in this shake. It tastes like a frozen Reese's Peanut Butter Cup in a glass.

MAKES 2 SHAKES

- **2 frozen bananas, peeled and cut into chunks**
- **2 tablespoons cocoa powder**
- **2 tablespoons natural peanut butter**
- **2 cups plant milk of your choice (soy, almond, cashew, etc.)**
- **½ cup water**

Place ingredients in a blender and blend for 30 seconds or until smooth. You may have to stop the blender a few times to stir before starting again.

VELVETY HOT CHOCOLATE

Simple and luxurious, I have been making this hot chocolate for years. It is a wonderful treat that can be whipped up in less than five minutes and is sure to cure your chocolate cravings. Using thicker milks like cashew or soy will give you a creamier drink.

SERVES 2

3-4 cups plant milk (cashew, almond, soy etc.) or enough for two mugs

2 tablespoons cocoa powder

1½ tablespoons maple syrup

Place all ingredients in a small saucepan and stir. Heat over medium heat until almost boiling and then remove from heat and whisk until smooth. Blend in a blender for a frothier finish.

VARIATIONS

Peppermint Hot Chocolate: add ¼ teaspoon peppermint extract

Gingerbread Hot Chocolate: add ½ teaspoon ground ginger

EVERYDAY GREEN SMOOTHIE

This is how I have been starting my day for years. This smoothie has a powerful energy boost that is cleansing and anti-inflammatory. The addition of lemon really cuts the intensity of the green taste. If green smoothies are new for you, start with a smaller handful of greens and build your way up to a larger amount over time.

SERVES 2

- Handful of leafy greens of your choice (spinach, romaine, collards, kale, chard etc.)
- 2½ cups water
- 2 bananas
- 1 apple or pear, cored
- ⅛ organic lemon, with peel
- 4 tablespoons hemp hearts (hemp seeds)
- 2 tablespoons chia seeds or ground flax seeds
- Small piece of fresh ginger root
- Tiny piece of turmeric root or ½ teaspoon ground turmeric

Add all ingredients to a blender and blend until smooth.

CHERRY VANILLA SHAKE

This thick and creamy shake makes a wonderful afternoon snack on a hot day. It also makes a satisfying dessert. Top it with Shake it up Coconut Whipped Cream (page 153) for a special treat.

MAKES 2 SHAKES

2 frozen bananas, peeled and cut into chunks

2½ cups vanilla-flavored plant milk of your choice (soy, almond, cashew etc.)

1½ cups frozen cherries

½ teaspoon pure vanilla extract

Place ingredients in a blender and blend for 30 seconds or until smooth. You may have to stop the blender a few times to stir before starting again.

NEAPOLITAN SHAKE

This colorful shake features a vanilla, chocolate and strawberry layer and is great fun for kids.

MAKES 2 SHAKES

3 frozen bananas, peeled and cut into chunks

2½ cups vanilla-flavored plant milk of your choice (soy, almond, cashew etc.)

½ cup frozen strawberries

1 tablespoon cocoa powder

½ teaspoon pure vanilla extract

Place the frozen banana chunks, plant milk and vanilla in a blender. Blend until smooth (you may have to stop and stir a few times). This is your vanilla base. Pour ⅔ from blender into a large measuring cup or bowl and set aside.

Add the frozen strawberries to the vanilla base remaining in the blender. Blend until smooth.

Spoon the strawberry layer into two glasses. This is the firmest and heaviest layer, so it will be the bottom layer.

Add approximately ½ of the vanilla base already set aside into each glass containing the strawberry layer to create the vanilla layer.

Rinse out the blender to remove the strawberry flavor and color. Pour the remaining vanilla base from your measuring cup or bowl into your blender and add the cocoa powder. Blend for a few seconds or until well mixed. Spoon chocolate layer on top of vanilla layer.

****SEE PHOTO ON PAGE 20.****

SOOTHING GOLDEN CHAI

A wonderful way to finish a meal or warm up on a cold night. Turmeric, ginger and cinnamon help reduce inflammation, making this an excellent choice for the body too. It's fun to watch the drink become more golden as the turmeric heats up.

SERVES 2

- **3-4 cups (or enough to fill two mugs) plant milk (soy, almond, cashew, etc.)**
- **1½ tablespoons maple syrup**
- **¼ -½ teaspoon ground turmeric (depending on how golden you like it)**
- **¼ teaspoon pure vanilla extract**
- **¼ teaspoon ground cinnamon**
- **¼ teaspoon ground ginger**
- **⅛ teaspoon ground cloves**
- **⅛ teaspoon ground cardamom**

Add all ingredients to a saucepan and stir. Bring almost to a boil over medium heat and then remove from heat and whisk until smooth.

Maple Pecan French Toast (page 10)

Chapter 2

BREAKFAST

POWER PACKED WELLNESS MUFFINS

I created this recipe for my friend Carol who loved muffins but had not had one in years because she was so turned off by the fat and sugar content in regular muffins. Healthy, moist and deeply satisfying, these muffins prove that eggs, sugar and excessive amounts of oil are unnecessary.

MAKES 12 MUFFINS

- **2 cups spelt or oat flour***
- **½ cup rolled oats**
- **2 teaspoons ground cinnamon**
- **2 teaspoons baking powder**
- **½ teaspoon baking soda**
- **¼ teaspoon sea salt**
- **¾ cup plant milk (rice, soy, almond etc.)**
- **1 tablespoon ground chia or flax seeds**
- **3 ripe bananas, mashed with fork or potato masher**
- **½ cup unsweetened applesauce**
- **½ cup raisins**
- **⅓ cup maple syrup**
- **¼ cup hemp hearts (hemp seeds)**
- **1 teaspoon pure vanilla extract**

Preheat oven to 375°F.

Prepare muffin tin: line it with papers or coat with a tiny amount of melted coconut oil in each compartment.

Mix the dry ingredients together in a medium sized bowl: flour, rolled oats, cinnamon, baking powder, baking soda, and salt and set aside.

Mix the ground chia or flax and the plant milk together in a small bowl and set aside.

In a large bowl, mix the mashed bananas, applesauce, raisins, maple syrup, hemp seeds, and vanilla and then add the plant milk and chia seed mixture. When well combined add the contents of the dry ingredient bowl and stir until just mixed.

Spoon batter into muffin tin and bake for 15 minutes.

* *Grind rolled oats in a coffee grinder, blender or food processor to make oat flour*

QUICK SOY YOGURT

An easy to make yogurt that can be spooned onto a bowl of granola or enjoyed on its own. Soy is health promoting, and it is important to always choose non-GMO tofu.

MAKES ABOUT 3 CUPS

20-ounces (600g) soft or silken tofu

¾ cup frozen orange juice concentrate

1 tablespoon pure vanilla extract

1 cup frozen or fresh fruit (e.g. blueberries, raspberries, strawberries)

Place the soft tofu, orange juice concentrate and vanilla into a blender or food processor. Blend until smooth. Pour into large bowl and stir in fruit. Store in fridge for up to a week.

CRANBERRY CRUNCH GRANOLA

Making your own granola means you can control the sugar and oil and avoid the overly sweet taste of commercial granola. The crunch in this granola comes from the wide variety of seeds, and the cranberry is just the right touch to brighten your cereal bowl and your morning.

MAKES ABOUT 5 CUPS

- **2½ cups rolled oats (not instant)**
- **¾ cup hemp hearts (hemp seeds)**
- **½ cup dry millet**
- **½ cup raw sunflower seeds**
- **½ cup unsweetened shredded coconut**
- **¼ cup chia seeds**
- **¼ cup chopped nuts (pecans, walnuts or almonds)**
- **½ teaspoon ground cinnamon**
- **½ teaspoon sea salt**
- **½ cup maple syrup**
- **3 tablespoons coconut oil, melted**
- **½ cup dried cranberries (add after baking)**

Preheat oven to 350°F.

In a large bowl, add the oats, hemp hearts, millet, sunflower seeds, coconut, chia seeds, nuts, cinnamon, and sea salt. Mix well. Drizzle with maple syrup and melted coconut oil and toss until well coated.

Spoon onto baking sheet lined with parchment paper and spread evenly. Bake for 30 minutes or until granola begins to brown. Remove from oven and gently stir in cranberries. Allow to cool fully on the baking sheet. When completely cool, transfer to airtight jar.

MAPLE PECAN FRENCH TOAST

This recipe uses tofu instead of eggs, and plant milk instead of dairy cutting the saturated fat and cholesterol while increasing the protein, fiber, minerals and vitamins. This is one of my favorite weekend breakfast treats.

SERVES 2

- **10-ounces (300g) soft or silken tofu**
- **½ cup plant milk (soy, rice, cashew, almond etc.)**
- **1 teaspoon ground cinnamon**
- **8 slices bread**
- **½ tablespoon coconut oil**
- **⅓ cup whole pecans**
- **2 bananas, sliced**
- **½ cup maple syrup**

Place the coconut oil in a non-stick frying pan and warm it up over medium heat. As it is warming blend the tofu, plant milk and cinnamon in a blender until smooth. Pour the mixture into a bowl and dip each slice of bread, one at a time making sure to coat both sides with the mixture and then place in the hot pan. Cook for about five to eight minutes or until the one side begins to brown. Flip and cook the other side.

To serve: top with pecans, sliced bananas and maple syrup.

****SEE PHOTO ON PAGE 34.****

SIMPLY DIVINE PANCAKES

These are simple and divine and when I am craving pancakes this is my go-to recipe. They are light and fluffy and easy to devour. Load them with fruit and nuts or dairy-free chocolate chips for a special brunch.

MAKES 6 PANCAKES (SERVES 2)

- **½ cup all-purpose flour**
- **½ cup spelt flour**
- **1 tablespoon baking powder**
- **¼ teaspoon sea salt**
- **1 cup plant milk (soy, almond, cashew etc.)**
- **1 tablespoon melted coconut oil**
- **1 tablespoon sugar**
- **1 teaspoon pure vanilla extract**
- **2-3 teaspoons sunflower oil for pan**

Mix the flour, baking powder and salt in a large bowl and set aside. In a medium sized bowl, mix the plant milk, melted coconut oil, sugar, and vanilla. Once well mixed, pour the liquid ingredients into the bowl containing the flour mixture. Stir until just mixed, careful not to over-stir so the pancakes stay fluffy.

Heat a griddle, non-stick pan or cast iron pan over medium heat until a drop of water sizzles when dropped into the pan. Add about one teaspoon sunflower oil and once hot, add pancake mix into pan using a ¼ cup measuring cup.

Cook for a few minutes until the bubbling at the surface stops, and flip. Cook for about two minutes on the other side. Remove from pan and cover to keep warm as you cook remaining pancakes.

Serve with maple syrup and top with berries, sliced bananas, walnuts, hemp seeds, etc.

TIP

Turn these into blueberry or chocolate chip pancakes by stirring in ½ cup frozen or fresh blueberries or ⅓ cup chocolate chips just before cooking.

CHEESY TOFU OMELET

This omelet is filling and delicious and always pleasantly surprises house guests who have never tried the vegan version of an omelet. Serve with a side salad and quinoa for dinner or a side of roasted potatoes and toast for a great brunch.

SERVES 2-3

1–14-ounce (400g) package firm or extra firm tofu*

2 tablespoons nutritional yeast

1 tablespoon low-sodium soy sauce

1 teaspoon ground turmeric

1 tablespoon coconut or vegetable oil

½ onion, finely chopped

½ red pepper, finely chopped

8 mushrooms, sliced

5 black olives, sliced

⅓ cup dairy free cheese shreds

Drain the tofu and mash by hand in a large bowl until crumbled. Mix in the nutritional yeast, soy sauce and turmeric and set aside.

Heat a frying pan over medium heat, adding the oil. Next add the onions, peppers and mushrooms. Sauté until the onions become translucent. Add the crumbled tofu mixture into the frying pan, mixing until well combined. Continue cooking for five to eight minutes. The turmeric will turn the tofu bright yellow as it cooks.

Flatten the tofu into the pan with a spatula and sprinkle the dairy free cheese on half of the tofu. Flip the non-cheesy side onto the cheesy side and press it down. Allow the omelet to cook for another few minutes so the cheese has a chance to melt.

* *Using firm or extra firm tofu is the key here. Avoid silken tofu, even if it is specified as firm silken tofu.*

BROCCOLI QUICHE WITH POTATO CRUST

The crust is made with one of my favorite foods in the world: potatoes. It amazes me how simple a potato crust is to make and it is the perfect base for this delicious quiche.

SERVES 6

CRUST:

3 large or 5 small potatoes

Pinch of sea salt

Pepper to taste

1-2 tablespoons extra virgin olive oil

FILLING:

1 tablespoon coconut oil

1 onion, minced

½ green pepper, chopped

10 button or cremini mushrooms, chopped

2 cloves garlic, minced

¾ cup broccoli florets, chopped

1–12-ounce (350g) package *medium firm* tofu (not silken)

1–12-ounce (350g) package *firm or extra firm* tofu (not silken)

2 tablespoons low-sodium soy sauce

2 tablespoons nutritional yeast

1 teaspoon ground turmeric

½ cup shredded non-dairy cheese

Preheat oven to 425°F.

Grate the potatoes and then press the moisture from the grated potatoes between a couple of kitchen towels. Add the grated potatoes to a 10-inch pie plate and drizzle with olive oil, salt and pepper. Use your hands to mix thoroughly and then press firmly into the pie plate to form a crust. Bake for 20-25 minutes or until the crust begins to brown.

While the crust is baking, melt the coconut oil in a large frying pan and add the onion, green pepper, mushrooms, broccoli, and garlic. Pan fry for 10 minutes over medium heat until onions are translucent. Drain the two packages of tofu and in a large bowl, mash them by hand until they are crumbled. Add in the soy sauce, nutritional yeast and turmeric. Add the tofu mix into the cooking vegetables, stirring to combine. Cook for several minutes until the tofu turns bright yellow from the warming turmeric. Remove from heat and add in the cheese. When the crust is ready, add in the filling pressing it firmly into the crust. Bake for 20–25 minutes or until the top begins to brown.

Chocolate Snowflake Snacks (page 52)

Chapter 3

SNACKS

OAHU ENERGY BITES

On my first trip to Hawaii, I spent time in the kitchen with nine-year-old Levi creating a new energy bite recipe. Levi made all the ingredient choices and the result is a perfectly sweet and energizing chocolate treat that kids (and adults) will love. Levi and his brothers need a lot of fuel when they are out surfing, and these energy bites are the perfect clean fuel for a day in the ocean. Levi lives on the island of Oahu and he came up with the name for this new creation

MAKES 12-15 ENERGY BITES

- **1 cup dates**
- **½ cup raw almonds, whole or sliced**
- **¼ cup natural peanut butter**
- **2 tablespoons chia seeds**
- **1 tablespoon cocoa powder**
- **½ teaspoon pure vanilla extract**
- **½ cup unsweetened shredded coconut**
- **¼ cup mini dairy-free chocolate chips**
- **¼ cup rolled oats**

Remove pits from the dates and add hot water to cover. Soak for 10 minutes to soften the dates. Drain the water from the dates and add the dates, almonds, peanut butter, chia seeds, cocoa powder, and vanilla extract to a blender. Blend until the dates are more like a date paste and the nuts are still a bit chunky. You may have to stop the blender a few times to stir and then start again.

Place blended ingredients in a large bowl and add the coconut, chocolate chips and rolled oats.

Mix all ingredients together with your hands until it becomes very sticky. Form small balls—the size of a large marble and store in the fridge or freezer. The balls will not freeze, they just become firmer in the freezer.

Option: Roll the balls in some extra shredded coconut before placing in the fridge

LEMON CRANBERRY COCONUT BITES

Sweet, tangy and beautiful. With the red cranberry accent, these bites are always a big hit.

MAKES ABOUT 20 BITES

16 big fresh dates (e.g. Medjool), pitted

Zest of 1 lemon

½ teaspoon pure vanilla extract

Pinch of sea salt

¼ cup hemp hearts (hemp seeds)

½ cup dried cranberries

½ cup unsweetened shredded coconut plus 2 tablespoons for rolling

Add dates, lemon zest, vanilla, and sea salt to a blender or food processor. Blend until dates have changed to a date paste. In a medium-sized bowl, add hemp hearts, cranberries and ½ cup coconut. Add in the date paste, mixing with hands until well combined. Roll a small amount of the mixture into a ball shape in your hands and then roll the ball in the extra coconut. Chill in the fridge or freezer.

CHOCOLATE SNOWFLAKE SNACKS

Keep these in the freezer for a cool treat during the hot days of summer.

MAKES 24 SNACKS

20 big fresh dates (e.g. Medjool), pitted

½ cup almonds

½ cup unsweetened shredded coconut plus 2 tablespoons for rolling

1 teaspoon pure vanilla extract

½ teaspoon sea salt

¼ cup cacao nibs or mini dairy-free chocolate chips

¼ cup cacao powder (or cocoa powder)

Place the almonds in a blender or food processor and process until fine. Remove and place in a bowl. Place the pitted dates, vanilla and sea salt in the blender or food processor and process until you have a date paste. Remove date paste and add it to the bowl with the fine almond pieces. Add remaining ingredients and stir together with your hands. Form small balls, rolling them between the palms of your hands. Roll the finished balls in the remaining coconut.

****SEE PHOTO ON PAGE 46.****

PEANUT BUTTER GRANOLA BARS WITH CHOCOLATE DRIZZLE

These divine granola bars are bursting with whole food nutrition and are firm enough to pack up for a hike without crumbling. The chocolate drizzle makes them extra special.

MAKES 12 BARS

BAR INGREDIENTS:

- **2 cups rolled oats**
- **½ cup unsweetened shredded coconut**
- **½ cup raw sunflower seeds**
- **½ cup natural peanut butter**
- **½ cup brown rice syrup**
- **½ cup dairy-free chocolate chips (optional)**
- **½ teaspoon pure vanilla extract**

CHOCOLATE DRIZZLE INGREDIENTS:

- **2 tablespoons coconut oil**
- **2 tablespoons cocoa powder or raw cacao powder**
- **2 tablespoons maple syrup**

OPTIONAL TOPPING:

Small handful of peanuts (chopped or whole)

Preheat oven to 375°F.

Mix the bar ingredients together in a large bowl. Don't be afraid to get right in there and mix everything up with your hands until it is well mixed and sticky. Press into a 11″ x 7″ baking pan lined with parchment paper. Bake for 25 minutes or until edges begin to brown. Allow to cool and then cut into bars.

Mix the drizzle ingredients together in a small saucepan and stir constantly over medium low heat until the oil is melted. Drizzle over the bars and if you like, top with the chopped or whole peanuts.

Allow the bars to set in the fridge for about 20 minutes.

OATMEAL BANANA BREAD SNACK CAKE

Is it a snack or is it a cake? Banana bread meets snack cake in this treat. Use dairy-free chocolate chips to make it irresistible for kids.

SERVES 8

WET INGREDIENTS:

- **5 ripe bananas, mashed**
- **1 flax egg***
- **½ cup maple syrup**
- **½ cup chopped walnuts or pecans**
- **⅓ cup cacao nibs or dairy free-chocolate chips (optional)**
- **1 tablespoon coconut oil, melted**
- **1 teaspoon pure vanilla extract**
- **1 teaspoon ground cinnamon**

DRY INGREDIENTS:

- **2½ cups oat flour (simply grind rolled oats in a coffee grinder or blender)**
- **1½ teaspoons baking powder**
- **½ teaspoon baking soda**
- **¼ teaspoon sea salt**

Preheat oven to 375°F and line a 9″ x 9″ baking pan with parchment paper.

* *To make a flax egg mix one tablespoon ground flax seeds with three tablespoons water and allow to sit for 10 minutes (ground chia seeds can also be used).*

Mix wet ingredients together in a large mixing bowl and add in the flax egg. Mix dry ingredients together in a medium sized mixing bowl. Stir dry ingredients into wet ingredients bowl until just mixed. Spoon mixture into parchment paper lined pan and bake for 30 minutes or until top starts to brown.

CHOCOLATE ALMOND ENERGIZERS

These little snacks are a great energy boost using simple whole foods. They keep well in the freezer, and they are perfect for those times when you feel the need for a chocolate energy boost.

MAKES 12-15 ENERGIZERS

½ cup raw almonds

6 big soft dates (e.g. Medjool), pitted

3 tablespoons hemp hearts (hemp seeds)

2 tablespoons cocoa powder

½ teaspoon pure vanilla extract

¼ teaspoon sea salt

Make sure you have taken the pits out of the dates and add all ingredients to your blender or food processor. Blend until the nuts are in small pieces and the mixture is sticking together nicely.

Remove from your blender or food processor (should be able to form a sticky ball by now) and place between two pieces of parchment paper. Press the ball down with your hands so it spreads out flat and is about ¼ inch thick. Use a rolling pin to complete the job.

Chill the mixture on the parchment paper for about an hour in the freezer. Then remove from freezer and cut into small squares with a pizza cutter or knife.

Store in the fridge or freezer (will not freeze solid).

Protein Super Salad (page 67)

Chapter 4

STARTERS & SALADS

NORI PEPPERONI STICKS

My friend John took a sniff inside the blender in one of my cooking classes and excitedly stated, "Oh my heavens, that smells like pepperoni!" I still smile when I think about that moment. The taste and smell we refer to as "pepperoni" is the perfect combination of spices used to enhance these delectable treats.

MAKES ABOUT 10 STICKS

- **1 cup sunflower seeds, soaked and drained**
- **¾ cup carrots, finely chopped**
- **1½ tablespoons miso paste**
- **1 clove garlic, chopped**
- **2 tablespoons lemon juice**
- **1 teaspoon onion powder**
- **½ teaspoon anise seeds**
- **½ teaspoon smoked paprika**
- **½ teaspoon peppercorns**
- **¼-½ teaspoon dried chili flakes (the more you add the hotter they get)**
- **4-5 sheets nori**

Preheat oven to 300°F.

Soak the sunflower seeds for two hours and then drain and rinse. Place all ingredients except for the nori into a food processor or blender and process until smooth.

Use a pair of scissors and cut the nori sheets in half (so each sheet is divided into two longer pieces). Spoon two heaping tablespoons of the mixture onto each half sheet. Smooth mixture into a solid line along the length of the sheet, one to two inches wide.

Roll up the stick starting with the edge closest to you that has the mixture on it. Wet the edge of the nori with a little water, before completing the roll. The moisture will help the roll stay closed.

Bake on a cookie sheet lined with parchment paper for 60 minutes. Allow to cool and enjoy.

HERBY SPELT CRACKERS

A delicious light and crispy cracker that can be modified with a few pinches of your favorite herbs to suit your taste buds.

MAKES ABOUT 4 DOZEN CRACKERS

- ¾ cup spelt flour or oat flour
- 1 cup all-purpose flour
- 2 tablespoons nutritional yeast
- 2 tablespoons sesame seeds
- 1 tablespoon sugar
- ½ teaspoon baking powder
- ½ teaspoon sea salt
- ¼ teaspoon dried basil
- ¼ teaspoon dried parsley
- ¼ teaspoon dried rosemary
- ¼ teaspoon garlic powder
- ¼ cup whole chia seeds
- ¾ cup plant milk
- 2 tablespoons extra virgin olive oil

Preheat oven to 325°F and cut two pieces of parchment paper to fit two baking sheets.

In a large bowl, mix the flours, nutritional yeast, sesame seeds, sugar, basil, parsley, rosemary (or whatever herbs you desire), garlic, baking powder, and sea salt; then, set aside. In a separate, medium-sized bowl, mix the chia seeds, plant milk and olive oil, allowing the mixture to sit for a few minutes until the chia seeds swell. Stir the chia mixture well and then add the wet mix into the bowl with the dry ingredients.

Use your hands to combine the ingredients until you have formed a nice ball. Divide the ball into two and place each one on one of the pieces of parchment paper. Add more flour to the surface of each ball to prevent sticking. Using a rolling pin, roll out the cracker dough into a large rectangle the size of the parchment paper. The dough should be very thin. Once rolled out, use a pizza cutter or knife to score the crackers into the shapes you'd like.

Bake for 20-25 minutes or until they begin to brown. Allow to cool and harden and then snap the crackers into individual pieces. Store in an airtight container.

MELTY NACHO DIP

My brother-in-law, Jody devoured this dip one Christmas and was shocked to later learn that it was made of beans and vegan cheese.

SERVES 4-6

- **1 cup cooked white beans**
- **1 garlic clove, minced**
- **½ teaspoon cumin**
- **½ teaspoon chili powder**
- **¼ teaspoon sea salt**
- **1½ cups prepared salsa**
- **Small handful of cilantro, chopped**
- **1 red pepper, finely chopped**
- **1 green pepper, finely chopped**
- **3 green onions, finely chopped**
- **1½ cups dairy free cheese shreds**

Heat oven to 350°F.

Prepare bean layer by mixing cooked white beans with garlic, cumin, chili powder, and salt in a blender or food processor until smooth. Add half the bean layer to the bottom of an oven-safe bowl. Next, add half of the salsa, and then half of the non-dairy cheese. Add half of the cilantro, green and red pepper, and green onions. Continue layering with remaining beans, salsa, cheese, peppers, cilantro, and green onions.

Bake for 25 minutes or until cheese is slightly melted. Serve with a big bowl of tortilla chips.

ROASTED SWEET POTATO HUMMUS

A new comforting twist on an old favorite, this hummus is bursting with flavor and nutrients and is also a lovely, cheerful color.

MAKES 3.5 CUPS

- **1 large sweet potato, chopped into cubes**
- **½ medium sized onion, chopped**
- **2 cloves garlic, skins removed**
- **3 cups cooked chickpeas**
- **¼ cup tahini**
- **3 tablespoons extra virgin olive oil (divided)**
- **3 tablespoons lemon juice**
- **1 teaspoon cumin**
- **1 teaspoon sea salt**
- **Pepper to taste**

Preheat oven to 425°F.

In a bowl, mix one tablespoon of olive oil with the onion, garlic and sweet potato. Transfer to a baking sheet lined with parchment paper and bake 30 minutes or until the sweet potato is tender and the edges are starting to brown.

In a food processor or blender, add the chickpeas, tahini, two tablespoons olive oil, lemon juice, cumin, salt and pepper, and the roasted veggies once they have come out of the oven and cooled. Blend until smooth and serve.

GORGEOUS GUACAMOLE

Avocados are incredibly nutrient dense and great for the body. Mix up some of this healthy dip and enjoy it with fresh veggies or tortilla chips.

MAKES ABOUT 2 CUPS

2 ripe avocados, skin and pits removed

1 clove garlic, minced

Juice of one lime (or lemon)

Pinch of sea salt

1 tomato, diced

1 green onion, minced

Place avocado in a medium sized bowl. Add garlic, lime and salt; mash with a fork. Stir in diced tomato, sprinkle green onion on top and serve.

SUN-DRIED TOMATO CASHEW CHEESE

Sun-dried tomatoes add a hint of color and flavor to this mouthwatering cheese. This cheese is soft and spreadable, and it plates beautifully.

SERVES 6-8

- **1 cup water**
- **1 teaspoon agar powder**
- **1 cup raw cashews**
- **¼ cup nutritional yeast**
- **½ teaspoon garlic powder**
- **¾ teaspoon sea salt**
- **2 tablespoons finely chopped sun-dried tomatoes (about 5 halves)**

Lightly oil six spaces in a standard muffin tin using a vegetable oil like olive or sunflower. You can use two to three small, oiled, ramekin-type bowls instead.

Place the cashews, nutritional yeast, garlic powder, and salt in a blender or food processor and pulse until you have a fine textured powder (do not blend until it becomes cashew butter).

Heat the water in a small saucepan to a boil and add the agar. Stir with a whisk and reduce the heat to a low simmer with a lid on for four minutes. Remove from heat and add the cashew mix into the agar and water mix, stirring with a whisk to fully combine. Then add the sun-dried tomatoes and stir to combine.

Spoon the mixture into the six muffin tins (or the ramekin-type bowls) and place in the fridge. Allow the cheese to set uncovered in the fridge for about an hour. Once set, turn the cheese onto a plate and enjoy!

TIPS

- Agar is a kind of seaweed and is the key to your success. It can be found in any health food store.
- If using dry sun-dried tomatoes, add them to a small pot of boiling water and allow them to sit for five minutes until soft. If using oil packed sun-dried tomatoes, rinse and chop.

MEXICAN QUINOA SALAD

A healthy and easy to make salad that is bursting with flavors. This is a great mid-week dinner that makes nice leftovers for lunches the following day.

SERVES 2-3 AS A MAIN DISH OR 4-6 AS A SIDE SALAD.

1½ cups quinoa, rinsed

3 cups water

1–15-ounce (440 ml) can black beans, drained and rinsed

1 cup frozen or fresh corn kernels

1 cup salsa

½ cup cilantro, chopped

1 red or green pepper, diced

½ teaspoon sea salt

Pepper to taste

2 avocados, sliced or cubed

Juice of 1 lime

Place quinoa and water in a pot, cover and bring to boil. Reduce to a simmer for 15-18 minutes or until all the water is absorbed.

Mix remaining ingredients in a large bowl and when quinoa is cooked add and stir. Serve with a squirt of lime juice on top. Can also be served cold.

TIP

Rinsing the quinoa is an important step as it removes the bitter tasting saponin which is the natural outer coating. Use a fine sieve and rinse several times for the best tasting quinoa.

PROTEIN SUPER SALAD

This one is for those who want it all: nuts, seeds, veggies, and legumes with a nice creamy dressing. I have been sharing this recipe with clients for many years and they always report back to me how much they love it.

SERVES 2 AS A MAIN DISH OR 4 AS A SIDE SALAD

1 avocado, chopped
1 tomato, chopped
1 red pepper, chopped
10 olives, black or green, chopped
3 green onions, chopped
1 cup cooked chickpeas
1 handful walnuts, chopped
2 cups baby spinach
2 tablespoons egg-free mayonnaise
Juice of 1 lemon
½ teaspoon sea salt
Pepper to taste
¼ cup raw pumpkin seeds

Place the avocado, tomato, red pepper, olives, green onions, chickpeas, walnuts, and spinach in a large bowl. In a separate small bowl, mix egg-free mayonnaise, lemon, salt, and pepper. Add to the salad and mix. Sprinkle each salad with pumpkin seeds.

****SEE PHOTO ON PAGE 56.****

MEDITERRANEAN QUINOA SALAD

A high protein, highly flavorful salad that can be served warm or cold.

SERVES 4 AS A SIDE OR 2 AS A MAIN DISH

- 1½ cups dry quinoa, rinsed
- 3 cups water
- ½ cup cooked chickpeas (if using canned, drain and rinse)
- 5 sun-dried tomatoes, finely chopped
- ½ cup hemp hearts (hemp seeds)
- 1 cup cucumber, diced
- ¼ cup red onion, diced
- 2 tablespoons capers
- 8 black olives, chopped
- Juice of 1 lemon
- ¼ teaspoon sea salt

Bring three cups of water to a boil in a covered pot. Add quinoa and reduce to a simmer keeping the pot covered. Cook 15-18 minutes or until water is absorbed.

Prepare remaining salad ingredients and mix them in a large bowl. Add hot quinoa and stir. Serve warm or allow quinoa to cool first and serve cool.

ARTICHOKE PASTA SALAD

This is a satisfying, protein rich salad that can easily become your main course.

SERVES 4 AS A MAIN DISH OR 8 AS A SIDE

- 2 cups dry rice pasta–elbows, rotini, spirals etc.
- 1–13-ounce (400 ml) can artichoke hearts, drained, rinsed and chopped
- 1 cup cooked chickpeas
- ½ cup cooked edamame beans, shelled
- Handful cilantro, chopped
- 2 green onions, sliced
- 2 tablespoons egg-less mayonnaise
- Juice of 1 lemon
- ½ teaspoon sea salt
- Pepper to taste

Cook pasta according to package directions and then rinse, drain and place in a large bowl. Add remaining ingredients to the large bowl and stir until evenly coated. Serve warm or cold.

TIP

Look for cooked edamame beans in the freezer section of your grocery store. Always choose non-GMO soy products.

WILD RICE CRANBERRY PECAN SALAD

Beautiful colors and a nice combination of crunchy, sweet and savoury tastes make this a wonderful salad or side dish. This one is always a hit in my cooking classes.

SERVES 4-6 AS A SIDE SALAD

1 cup wild rice mix

2½ cups water

½ cup dried cranberries

½ cup pecans, toasted and then chopped*

3 sliced green onions

½ lemon juiced

1 tablespoon maple syrup

Salt and pepper to taste

Add rice and water to a medium sized pot and cover with a lid. Bring to a boil, reduce heat and simmer for 30 minutes or until all the water is absorbed. In a separate bowl, mix the remaining ingredients. When the rice is cooked, add into the bowl, mixing everything together. Can be served warm or cold.

* *Toast pecans in a dry frying pan over medium heat for five minutes or until they become fragrant. Stir often to avoid burning the pecans. Once they are toasted and have cooled, chop them into large pieces.*

SASSY KALE MANGO SALAD

This one is sassy because it has so much flavor. Garlic, ginger, lime and a bit of heat with the red pepper flakes make an amazing dressing.

SERVES 3 AS A MAIN DISH OR 6 AS A SIDE

1 bunch kale, de-stemmed
Juice of one lemon
¼ teaspoon sea salt

DRESSING:

½ cup almond butter or tahini
¼ cup water
Juice and zest of 1 lime
1 garlic clove, minced
½-inch fresh ginger, minced
2 dates, pitted
1 tablespoon low-sodium soy sauce or tamari
Pinch of red pepper flakes

TOPPERS:

2 small mangos peeled and chopped
1 red pepper, chopped
1 cup cherry tomatoes, cut in half

Cut kale into small pieces and toss in a bowl with lemon juice and sea salt. Massage with hands for one to two minutes until kale shrinks and becomes glossy. Mix the dressing in a blender or food processor and pour over kale. Mix well. Top with mango, red pepper and cherry tomatoes.

TIP

The easiest way to de-stem kale is to hold the base of the stem with one hand and firmly slide your other hand up the stem pulling off the leafy parts as you slide.

SAVE THE TUNA SALAD

I grew up eating a lot of tuna sandwiches. What I missed most when I went vegan was the combination of creamy dressing with the celery and pickle. This recipe makes it possible to have it all without causing harm to anyone.

MAKES A SALAD FOR 3-4 OR 4 SANDWICHES

- **1–15-ounce (440 ml) can chickpeas, drained and rinsed**
- **2 tablespoons egg-free mayonnaise**
- **½ tablespoon low-sodium soy sauce**
- **1 stalk celery, minced**
- **1 dill pickle, minced**
- **2 tablespoons red onion, minced**
- **Pepper to taste**
- **8 slices of bread or 3 cups salad greens**

Mash chickpeas in a bowl with a potato masher, then add egg-free mayonnaise, soy sauce, celery, pickle, onion, and pepper. Serve on a bed of fresh salad greens, or as a sandwich filling with bread or rolls.

SUPER SLAW WITH CREAMY TAHINI DRESSING

This slaw requires a bit more chopping, but the result is worth it. The colors and flavors are delectable, and the nutrient density is high.

SERVES 8 AS A SIDE SALAD

2 cups finely sliced red cabbage
2 cups finely sliced green cabbage
1 cup shredded carrots
1 cup finely shredded kale (stems removed)
1 cup beets, cut into fine matchsticks
1 apple, cut into fine matchsticks
½ red onion, minced
¼ cup chopped fresh parsley
½ cup toasted sunflower seeds
¼ cup toasted sesame seeds

DRESSING:
4 tablespoons tahini
2 cloves garlic, minced
Juice of 1 lemon
2 tablespoons apple cider vinegar
1 tablespoon maple syrup
1 tablespoon water
1 tablespoon prepared mustard
Sea salt and pepper to taste

Place the slaw ingredients in a large bowl and whisk the dressing together in a separate bowl. Mix the dressing into the slaw and serve.

Allowing the salad to sit for about 30 minutes before serving will marinate the flavors.

PECAN CAESAR SALAD

Move over croutons!
Toasted pecans are a delicious replacement in this creamy salad.

SERVES 4 AS A SIDE SALAD

- 1 head romaine lettuce, chopped into bite-sized pieces
- ½ cup water
- ⅓ cup sunflower seeds
- 1 tablespoon tahini
- Juice of one lemon
- 2 garlic cloves, minced
- 1 fresh date (e.g. Medjool), pitted
- 1 teaspoon miso paste
- Pepper to taste
- ¼ cup raw pecans

Place chopped romaine in a large bowl. Toast pecans in a dry frying pan over medium heat for five minutes or until they become fragrant. Stir often to prevent burning. Prepare dressing by combining remaining ingredients in a blender or food processor. Blend until smooth.

Pour dressing over romaine lettuce and top with toasted pecans.

CHUNKY
POTATO SALAD

This is your classic potato salad made without the cruelty of eggs. Cut the potatoes into big chunks to make this simple creamy salad really stand out.

SERVES 4-6 AS A SIDE SALAD

5-6 potatoes, cut into chunks
⅓ cup egg-free mayonnaise
3 green onions, minced
Salt and pepper to taste

Boil potatoes in a big pot of water. When they are soft, but not mushy (test with fork), drain them and set aside to cool. When cool, transfer potatoes to a large bowl adding in egg free mayonnaise, green onion, salt, and pepper to taste.

heesy Cashew Collard Wraps (page 89)

Chapter 5

SOUPS & SANDWICHES

CREAM OF CELERY SOUP

The potatoes and coconut milk create a comforting and creamy finish. You only need a pinch of salt in this recipe because celery has a lot of naturally occurring sodium.

SERVES 6

- **1 head of celery (about 12 stalks), finely chopped**
- **1 large white or yellow onion, chopped**
- **1 tablespoon extra virgin olive oil**
- **6 cups water**
- **1 bay leaf**
- **3 white potatoes, chopped**
- **½ teaspoon thyme**
- **½ teaspoon dried dill**
- **½ teaspoon of sea salt (try roasted garlic salt page 106)**
- **1–13-ounce (400 ml) can full fat coconut milk**
- **¼ cup fresh dill or fresh parsley, chopped (optional)**

Heat olive oil in large soup pot over medium heat and add chopped onion and celery. Sauté until onions are clear.

Add water, potatoes, bay leaf, thyme, dill, and salt and bring to a boil. Cover and reduce heat to a simmer for 30 minutes.

Remove from heat, locate and remove the bay leaf. Add the coconut milk and transfer to a blender. Blend until creamy and serve into bowls, topping with optional fresh dill or parsley.

ROASTED CAULIFLOWER SOUP

A truly memorable soup that quickly became my mother's new favorite. The roasted veggies give the soup a flavourful depth. Blending the soup makes it nice and creamy.

SERVES 4

- **1 head of cauliflower cut into florets**
- **3 large potatoes, cubed**
- **2 garlic cloves, minced**
- **1 onion, chopped**
- **1 tablespoon extra virgin olive oil**
- **3 cups of vegetable broth or water**
- **1 teaspoon garam masala or mild curry powder**
- **1 teaspoon sea salt**
- **Pepper to taste**
- **1 cup plant milk (rice, soy, almond, cashew etc.)**

Preheat oven to 425°F.

Place cauliflower, potatoes, garlic, and onions in a roasting pan or on a baking sheet lined with parchment paper and drizzle olive oil over top. Stir until all the vegetables are nicely coated in olive oil. Roast uncovered for 30 minutes in the oven.

Once cooked, place roasted veggies into large soup pot and add the vegetable broth or water, salt, pepper, and garam masala and bring to a boil. Reduce heat and simmer for 10 minutes. Remove from heat and stir in the plant milk. Pour soup into a blender and blend until smooth. Return the blended soup to the pot and simmer for another 10 minutes.

COMFORTING CARROT PEANUT SOUP

My friends, Kathseva and Andrew, served me a wonderful carrot peanut soup at their retreat center a few years ago. With their guidance, I replicated the recipe at home. Despite its simplicity, this soup is a real treat with its natural sweetness and creamy finish.

SERVES 6

6 cups water
2 sweet potato, diced
5 carrots, diced
2 teaspoons cumin
1 teaspoon sea salt
4 tablespoons natural peanut butter

Bring water to a boil in a large pot and add sweet potato, carrots, cumin, and salt. Reduce heat to a simmer and cook for 25 minutes. Stir in peanut butter and cook for another five minutes. Carefully place the hot soup in a blender and blend until smooth.

RED LENTIL SOUP

This is my number one comfort food soup. There is a tasty blend of savory herbs and spices with lots of garlic, and the red lentils thicken it up nicely.

SERVES 4-6

2 cups dry red lentils
1 large yellow onion, diced
2 carrots, diced
6 cloves garlic, minced
4 cups vegetable broth
4 cups water
2 bay leaves
1 teaspoon oregano
1 teaspoon rosemary
1 teaspoon pepper
1 teaspoon sea salt
½ teaspoon thyme

Add all ingredients to a large pot, cover and bring to a boil. Reduce to a simmer and allow to simmer for 30 minutes. Remove bay leaves and serve.

TOASTED VEGGIE WRAPS

With the cheesiness of hummus and avocado, the crunch of carrots and cabbage, and the warmth of a toasted wrap, these sandwiches are a hit with adults and kids alike. A great way to satisfy your hunger while getting a big dose of veggies.

MAKES 2 WRAPS

1 cup grated red or green cabbage
1 cup spinach
2 carrots, grated
4 tablespoons hummus
1 avocado, cut into slices
2 whole grain tortilla wraps

Preheat oven or toaster oven to 350°F.

Prepare the vegetables and set aside. Spread two tablespoons of hummus into each wrap. Add half of the vegetables to each wrap and close like a burrito, making sure to fold the ends in. Bake for 10 minutes or until the wrap begins to brown.

EGG-LESS SALAD SANDWICHES

I love this recipe and I am always amazed at how much this egg salad tastes like what I remember eating as a kid. The best thing about this recipe is that not only is it delicious, no animals were harmed.

MAKES 4 SANDWICHES

1–14-ounce (400g) block firm tofu, drained and mashed by hand

2 tablespoons low-sodium soy sauce

2 tablespoons nutritional yeast

1 teaspoon ground turmeric

¼ cup white or yellow onion minced

1 teaspoon maple syrup

4 tablespoons egg free mayonnaise

8 slices of bread

Handful of lettuce

Pan fry the tofu with soy sauce, nutritional yeast and turmeric in a dry frying pan until nice and yellow (about five minutes). Transfer to a large bowl and add onions, maple syrup and egg free mayo. Stir until mixed. Serve on bread with lettuce.

CHEESY CASHEW COLLARD WRAPS

Collard leaves make incredible wraps because they are both sturdy and flexible. This recipe blanches the leaves to make them soft and pliable, you can also use raw leaves for a crunchier wrap.

MAKES 6 WRAPS

1 cup raw cashews, soaked for 2 hours, then drained
¼ -½ cup water
Juice of ½ lemon
1 clove garlic, minced
1 tablespoon nutritional yeast
½ teaspoon sea salt
Pinch of black pepper
6 large collard leaves
1 red, yellow or orange bell pepper, cut into thin slices
1 cucumber, cut into thin slices
1 mango, peeled and cut into thin slices
1 avocado, cut into thin slices
1–3.5 ounce (100g) package of alfalfa sprouts

Prepare cashew cheese spread by placing soaked cashews in a food processor or blender. Add ¼ cup water, garlic, nutritional yeast, salt, pepper, lemon juice, and blend until creamy consistency is reached (adding more water if needed). Place cheese spread in a bowl and set aside.

Fill a large pot halfway with water and bring to a boil.

Remove the bottom ¾ of each collard leaf stem from each of the collard leaves and place all six leaves in the boiling water, adding the lid and boil for one minute. Remove from the boiling water and rinse under cold water to stop the cooking process.

Place the leaves on kitchen towels to dry. One at a time lay the collard leaves flat on the counter, slightly overlapping each one at the space where the stem is missing. Fill with cashew cheese spread, veggies, sprouts, and mango and roll like a burrito. Cut diagonally and serve.

PAN-FRIED TOFU SANDWICHES

I make these sandwiches at least once a week in our home. They are easy, delicious and filling. In my cooking classes, people often think the tofu tastes like fried eggs once it has been cooked in the soy sauce and nutritional yeast.

MAKES 2 SANDWICHES

½–14-ounce (400g) block firm or extra firm tofu (not silken)

2 tablespoons low-sodium soy sauce

2 tablespoons nutritional yeast

4 slices bread

2 tablespoons egg free mayonnaise

Small handful greens (spinach, romaine etc.)

Open the tofu package and let the water drain. Cut half the tofu block into thin slices (about eight slices) and place in a frying pan over medium heat. Pour the soy sauce over the cooking tofu. Sprinkle the tofu with the nutritional yeast. Flip the tofu slices after five minutes and cook the other side for another five minutes.

Place half of the cooked slices on each sandwich and dress with egg-free mayo and greens.

Cashew Sour Cream (page 97)

Chapter 6

SAUCES, DRESSINGS & MORE

GREEN GODDESS DRESSING

This green, lean and not so mean dressing is a taste sensation that makes any salad or dinner bowl come to life. Tahini is wonderful in dressings because it is a creamy whole food that is calcium-rich.

MAKES ABOUT 1.5 CUPS

- **½ cup tahini**
- **½ cup water**
- **½ cup chopped parsley**
- **1 lemon, juiced**
- **1 lime, juiced**
- **½ red onion, minced**
- **2 garlic cloves, minced**
- **2 big fresh dates, pitted or 2 teaspoons maple syrup**
- **2 tablespoons tamari or low-sodium soy sauce**
- **½ tablespoon cumin**

Blend everything in a blender until smooth.

TIP

Use this as a dressing cold, or warm it up gently in a saucepan to use as a sauce to top bowls of steamed veggies or rice.

CHEESY SUNFLOWER SEED DRESSING

This is a cheesy dressing that sticks to your greens, and leaves you feeling like a salad really can be a full meal.

MAKES ABOUT 1 CUP

½ cup sunflower seeds (*soaked if possible)
½ cup water
Juice of ½ lemon
1 date, pitted, or 1 teaspoon maple syrup
2 tablespoons nutritional yeast
1 tablespoon dried basil
¼ teaspoon sea salt

Place all ingredients in a blender or food processor and blend until creamy.

* *If you have time, soak the sunflower seeds and you will get a creamier dressing. Place the seeds in a bowl with water for two hours and then drain them.*

CASHEW SOUR CREAM

Four-ingredient sour cream that will truly amaze you. Dollop it onto baked potatoes or drizzle it over the Big Burrito Bowl (page 130) for an incredible finish.

MAKES ABOUT 1.5 CUPS

- **1 cup soaked cashews*, drained**
- **½ cup water**
- **1½ teaspoons apple cider vinegar**
- **¼ teaspoon salt**

Blend well until smooth in a blender or food processor.

* *Soak cashews for four hours or overnight by covering them with water.*

****SEE PHOTO ON PAGE 92.****

NANCY ZYLSTRA'S GORGEOUS GRAVY

Nancy Zylstra and her daughter Awna, died on August 31, 2005 in a car collision, near Bancroft, Ontario. Nancy was a dedicated animal activist who lived on, and operated the beautiful Pinecone Forest Nature Sanctuary with her daughter Awna and her husband Gus. Nancy kindly shared her mouthwatering gravy recipe with me back in 2001 when I was just starting my vegan journey. Memories of her cooking style continue to influence me in the kitchen to this day. This gravy is frequently made in my household and compliments my Shepherd's Seed Pie (page 132), Roasted Wedge Poutine (page 112) and Stuffed Tofu Roast (page 141). Nancy's memory lives on with this scrumptious recipe.

MAKES ABOUT 3 CUPS

8 tablespoons vegetable oil (sunflower, safflower etc.)

4 cloves garlic, minced

8 tablespoon flour (oat, brown rice, all-purpose etc.)

3 tablespoons tamari

2 tablespoons nutritional yeast

2¾ cups water

1 tablespoon poultry seasoning (this is an innocent pre-packaged mixture of sage, rosemary, thyme, marjoram etc.)

Pepper to taste

Heat the oil in a medium saucepan over medium heat and when hot, add the minced garlic. Sauté for two to three minutes. Remove from heat and add flour, nutritional yeast and tamari, mixing with a whisk to form a paste. Slowly add water, using the whisk to incorporate until smooth. Don't worry if there are a few lumps. Add the poultry seasoning and pepper. Place back on low heat for 10 minutes stirring often and add more water if too thick.

TIP

If you would like a lighter version of this gravy, use water instead of oil when sautéeing the garlic.

CREAMY PEANUT SAUCE

Simple and flavorful, warmed up this sauce will charm your noodles, rice or veggies. It also makes a great dip.

MAKES 1 CUP

½ cup natural peanut butter
¼ cup water
Juice of ½ lemon
2 teaspoons pure maple syrup
2 teaspoons tamari or low-sodium soy sauce
1 clove crushed garlic
½ teaspoon grated fresh ginger

Place all ingredients in a deep bowl and whisk together. If it's too thick, add more water. Store in the refrigerator in a sealed container for up to five days.

SWEET AND SOUR SAUCE

Use this sauce on a veggie stir-fry for a fast and delicious take-out experience.

MAKES ABOUT 1.5 CUPS

- **1 cup pineapple juice**
- **¼ cup water**
- **¼ cup rice vinegar**
- **2 tablespoons ketchup**
- **2 tablespoons maple syrup or brown sugar**
- **1 tablespoon tamari or low-sodium soy sauce**
- **1 tablespoon arrowroot powder**

Combine all ingredients in a medium sized saucepan with a whisk and cook over medium-low heat for about five minutes. The sauce will thicken as it cooks.

HANDMADE TARTAR SAUCE

I have always loved tartar sauce and I thought that making my own would be hard. Turns out it's extremely easy, and it tastes so good! Try it on the Fishless Fillets (page 129).

MAKES ABOUT 1/2 CUP

½ cup egg-free mayonnaise

1 tablespoon sweet pickle relish

1 teaspoon lemon juice

½ teaspoon prepared mustard

Pinch of salt and pepper

Place all ingredients in a bowl and mix with a spoon.

VEGAN BUTTER

My favorite store brand vegan butter uses palm oil, which because of the destruction it causes to animals and the earth, is not appealing to me. I started making my own butter instead and it's absolutely delicious. This creamy butter is great on toast, in baking, and anywhere you would normally use butter.

MAKES ALMOST 2 CUPS

¼ cup plant milk (almond, soy, cashew, rice etc.)

1 teaspoon apple cider vinegar

½ teaspoon sea salt

¾ cup refined* coconut oil, just melted

½ cup olive or sunflower oil

1 teaspoon soy or sunflower lecithin granules (in the refrigerated section of your natural food store)

¼ teaspoon ground turmeric (optional for a deeper yellow colour)

Place the plant milk, apple cider vinegar and salt in a small bowl and whisk together. Let it sit for about 10 minutes.

Melt the coconut oil so it's just barely melted and as close to room temperature as possible. Place it in a blender and add the olive or sunflower oil. Add in the plant milk mixture, lecithin, turmeric (if using) and blend for 30 seconds. Pour the mixture into a mold—like an ice cube tray or a two-cup capacity freezer-safe glass bowl with lid—and place it in the freezer to solidify. The butter should be ready to use in about an hour. Store it in an airtight container in the refrigerator for up to one month.

* *Be sure to use refined coconut oil, not unrefined coconut oil. The unrefined coconut oil, while still a great product, will make your butter taste like coconuts.*

TIP

If you choose to use soy lecithin, be sure that you choose a brand that is non-GMO.

VEGAN PARMESAN

Imagine making a healthy, compassionate and delicious batch of parmesan in about 20 seconds. Spoon liberally over pasta, pizza, noodles, popcorn or anything needing some cheesy love.

MAKES 1/3 CUP

¼ cup nutritional yeast

¼ cup hemp hearts or sesame seeds

Pinch of salt (optional)

Grind together for about 20 seconds in a food processor, blender or coffee grinder.

TIP

Nutritional yeast is a tasty non-active yeast that has a flaky texture and a cheesy, nutty flavor. Depending on the manufacturer, it is often incredibly high in B12 as well, making it a tasty vitamin superstar. Find it in health food stores and in bulk food stores.

ROASTED GARLIC SALT

This salt infusion is a fantastic way to add the rich flavor of roasted garlic into any dish that benefits from salt. Use it in unlimited ways in soups or sauces, guacamole, hummus or noodle dishes.

MAKES 1 CUP

- **1 medium sized garlic bulb (about 10 cloves)**
- **½ teaspoon extra virgin olive oil**
- **1 cup fine sea salt**

Preheat oven to 400°F.

Break open garlic bulb and peel each garlic clove. Place the cloves in aluminum foil and drizzle with olive oil. Close the aluminum foil, creating a sealing packet, and place on the center rack of the oven. Bake for 40 minutes.

Once roasted, remove the garlic packet and reduce oven temperature to 200°F. Remove the roasted garlic cloves from the foil and place them in a blender or food processor with the salt. Pulse or slowly blend until the garlic is integrated into the salt and there are no longer any garlic pieces visible.

Transfer the garlic salt onto a baking sheet lined with parchment paper and bake for 20 minutes at 200°F to dry the salt.

Remove and allow to cool and then place in an airtight container.

SMOKY ALL-DRESSED SEA SALT

This is the perfect salt blend to sprinkle on popcorn, mac and cheese, potato wedges or sweet potato fries.

MAKES ABOUT 3/4 CUP

- **½ cup fine sea salt**
- **5 tablespoons nutritional yeast**
- **2 teaspoons dried parsley flakes**
- **1 teaspoon chili powder**
- **1 teaspoon garlic powder**
- **1 teaspoon onion powder**
- **1 teaspoon smoked paprika**
- **½ teaspoon black pepper**

Mix all ingredients together in a bowl and then place in an airtight jar.

Brussels Sprouts with Pomegranate Seeds (page 115)

Chapter 7

SIDES

MAPLE-ROASTED SQUASH

As far as veggies go, I think roasted squash is the ultimate comfort food. Adding a bit of maple syrup highlights the natural sweetness and makes it that much better.

SERVES 6-8 AS A SIDE

- **2 acorn, buttercup, or butternut squash (cut in half and seeds scooped out)**
- **4 tablespoons maple syrup**
- **2 tablespoons coconut oil, melted**
- **1 teaspoon sea salt**

Preheat oven to 400°F.

Mix the melted coconut oil, maple syrup and salt in a small bowl. Place the squash halves in a baking pan with the cut sides up. Using your hands, coat the inside of each squash half with the maple syrup mixture. Cover with aluminum foil and roast for 30 minutes. Remove the foil and roast until tender, about another 20-30 minutes.

LEMON PARSLEY GREEN BEANS

These beans are beautifully fragrant, crunchy and lemony. A favorite in my cooking classes.

SERVES 6-8 AS A SIDE

1½ pounds green beans, ends trimmed off

3 tablespoons extra virgin olive oil

2 large garlic cloves, minced

¼ cup chopped fresh parsley

¼ cup sesame seeds

1 tablespoon lemon zest

Sea salt and pepper to taste

Steam beans in large covered pot with about two inches of water until crisp tender, about four to six minutes. Drain well.

In heavy large skillet over medium-high heat, add olive oil. Once hot, add garlic and stir for 30 seconds. Add beans and sauté until heated through, about five minutes. Stir in sesame seeds, parsley and lemon zest. Season with salt and pepper and serve while hot.

TIP

Weigh the beans in the grocery store so it's easy to bring home exactly 1½ pounds.

ROASTED POTATO WEDGE POUTINE

It doesn't get more Canadian than this! Poutine usually has dairy cheese curds and beefy gravy, both of which are easily replaced in this recipe.

SERVES 4 AS A SIDE OR 2 LARGE PORTIONS

4 large potatoes

1 tablespoon vegetable oil (sunflower, safflower, etc.)

½ teaspoon sea salt

¾ cup dairy-free cheese

2 cups Nancy Zylstra's Gorgeous Gravy (page 98)

Preheat oven to 425°F.

If using organic potatoes, simply wash skins and pat dry the potatoes. If using non-organic, peel the potatoes first. Cut potatoes into thick wedges (one large potato should make eight wedges). Place in a bowl and drizzle with oil. Add salt and stir until well coated. Place on a baking sheet and bake for 30 minutes or until soft when a fork is inserted, and the wedges are beginning to brown.

While potato wedges are roasting, prepare Nancy Zylstra's Gorgeous Gravy. When the wedges are roasted, add eight to a plate (if making four side dishes of poutine) or 16 to a plate (if making two larger portions). Cover with a portion of cheese and top with gravy.

ALL-DRESSED CHEESY SWEET POTATO FRIES

These sweet potato fries are bursting with flavor. They make a perfect sidekick for veggie burgers.

SERVES 4 AS A SIDE

4 sweet potatoes

2 tablespoons vegetable oil (sunflower, safflower etc.)

3 tablespoons nutritional yeast

1 teaspoon sea salt

1 teaspoon garlic powder

1 teaspoon onion powder

½ teaspoon chili powder

¼ teaspoon black pepper

Preheat oven to 375°F.

Cut sweet potatoes into French fry shape and place in a large bowl. Drizzle oil over fries and then sprinkle nutritional yeast, salt, garlic powder, onion powder, chili powder, and pepper over the fries. Mix to thoroughly coat.

Place the fries on a baking sheet and bake 20-25 minutes or until sweet potatoes are soft and starting to brown.

BRUSSELS SPROUTS WITH POMEGRANATE SEEDS

Bring your baby cabbages to life with just a hint of sea salt and the sweetness of pomegranate seeds.

SERVES 8 AS A SIDE

4 cups of Brussels sprouts, ends trimmed off and cut in half

1½ tablespoons melted coconut oil or sunflower oil

½ teaspoon sea salt

Seeds of one pomegranate

Preheat the oven to 425°F.

Place the cut Brussels sprouts in a bowl and drizzle with oil. Mix and then add salt, mixing again. Place in a casserole dish and cover with a lid, baking for 25-30 minutes, or until the Brussels sprouts are soft when poked with a fork and starting to brown.

Remove from oven, stir in pomegranate seeds and serve.

****SEE PHOTO ON PAGE 108.****

ROASTED GARLIC ROSEMARY POTATOES

These little gems are sure to please everyone at brunch or dinner time. They are bursting with the flavors of garlic and rosemary and are crispy brown on the edges.

SERVES 4 AS A SIDE

1½ pounds small red or white potatoes

2-3 tablespoons extra virgin olive oil

3 garlic cloves, minced

2 tablespoons fresh rosemary, minced (or 2 teaspoons dried)

¾ teaspoon sea salt

Pepper to taste

Preheat the oven to 425°F.

Cut the potatoes in half and place in a bowl. Drizzle the olive oil and add the garlic, rosemary, salt, and pepper. Toss until potatoes are well coated. Place potatoes on baking sheet and roast for one hour flipping twice along the way.

MISO BUTTER TURNIPS

Turnips may become your new favorite side dish once you try this recipe. Braised with browning edges and the tang of miso, this might simply be what it takes to get the family to love this amazing root vegetable.

SERVES 4-6 AS A SIDE DISH

- **1 large turnip, peeled and cut into small chunks**
- **2 tablespoons Vegan Butter (page 104) or coconut oil, divided**
- **1 cup vegetable broth (or more if needed)**
- **2 tablespoons miso paste**
- **1 teaspoon maple syrup or sugar**

Heat one tablespoon of the Vegan Butter in a deep skillet and add the turnip chunks. Cook over medium heat for about 10 minutes or until the turnips begin to brown along the edges. Add the vegetable broth and maple syrup and reduce heat to a simmer. Allow to simmer uncovered for about 20 minutes or until the turnip is soft when pierced with a fork and the vegetable broth has dissipated. Add more broth if the pan gets dry before turnips are soft.

While the turnips are simmering, mix the remaining tablespoon of Vegan Butter and miso in a small bowl and set aside.

Once the turnips are soft, remove the skillet from the heat and gently stir in the miso butter.

SAVORY STUFFING

The perfect holiday meal side dish that is great on its own or stuffed in a tofu roast.

SERVES 8

- 1 onion, chopped
- 3 tablespoons Vegan Butter (page 104) or coconut oil
- 1 green pepper, finely chopped
- 10 mushrooms, sliced
- 4 stalks of celery, finely chopped
- 2 cloves of garlic, minced
- ½ loaf of rye or your favorite bread toasted and cut into small cubes
- 1 cup vegetable broth
- 3 tablespoons tamari
- 1½ teaspoons poultry seasoning
- Pepper to taste

Heat a large frying pan over medium heat and sauté the onion in Vegan Butter or oil until the onion is clear. Stir in the green pepper, mushrooms, celery, and garlic. Cook for a few minutes and then add the cubed bread, vegetable broth, tamari, poultry seasoning, and pepper. Continue to sauté until the bread absorbs all the moisture. Remove from heat and cover with foil to retain moisture before serving.

Big Burrito Bowl (page 130)

Chapter 8

MAINS

SWEET POTATO CHILI

Chili with a sweet side. The corn and sweet potatoes are a perfect match for a mild heat in this chili.

SERVES 4-6

- 2 cups water
- 1–28-ounce (796 ml) can chopped tomatoes
- 1–13-ounce (398 ml) can kidney beans, drained and rinsed
- 1 large onion, chopped
- 1 large sweet potato, cut into small cubes
- 2 carrots, chopped
- 1 cup corn kernels
- 2 cloves garlic, minced
- 2 tablespoons mild chili powder
- 1 teaspoon cumin
- 1 teaspoon sea salt
- Pepper to taste

Place all ingredients in a large pot, cover with a lid and bring to a boil. Reduce the heat and simmer for 25-30 minutes or until the sweet potatoes are soft, stirring occasionally. Top with Gorgeous Guacomole (page 64).

MUSHROOM STROGANOFF

I created this recipe for my partner who loved stroganoff as a child. She says her mother, Christine made an amazing stroganoff, and this recipe reminds her so much of that one. It is a creamy dish that is bursting with intense mushroom flavor.

SERVES 4-6

2 cups dry, eggless, flat noodles or brown rice spirals

½ tablespoon coconut oil

1 large onion, chopped

1 pound mushrooms cut into chunks or thick slices (about 6 cups)

2 cups vegetable broth

2 tablespoons tomato sauce

2 tablespoons low-sodium soy sauce or tamari

1 teaspoon poultry seasoning (or ½ teaspoon dried thyme and ½ teaspoon dried sage)

3 tablespoons flour (e.g. brown rice, spelt flour etc.) with ¼ cup water

1–14-ounce (400 ml) can full fat coconut milk

Freshly ground black pepper to taste

¼ cup fresh parsley, finely chopped

Cook the noodles according to the package directions, undercooking them slightly as they will be cooked a little bit more later in the recipe. Drain, rinse and set aside.

In a large deep frying pan, melt the coconut oil over medium heat, and then add the onions. Cook for two to three minutes, and then add the mushrooms, broth, tomato sauce, soy sauce, and poultry seasoning. Bring to a simmer and cook, uncovered for 15 minutes, stirring occasionally.

Whisk the flour with ¼ cup water in a small bowl and then add the mixture into the pan, stirring to combine. Continue stirring the stroganoff for a few more minutes until the sauce begins to thicken. Stir in the coconut milk and the cooked noodles and cook for another three minutes. Add black pepper and sprinkle with parsley to serve.

1896

CREAMY VEGETABLE STEW

This stew smells wonderful as it cooks with all the rich spices. The coconut milk added at the end makes the stew nice and creamy and will leave you feeling deeply satisfied.

SERVES 6-8

2 cups water
1–28-ounce (796 ml) can tomatoes, whole or chopped
1 cup cooked chickpeas
½ cup dry red lentils
1 onion, chopped
1 sweet potato, cubed
1 bulb fennel, diced
1 cup cabbage, chopped
2 carrots, finely chopped
6 mushrooms, chopped
1 teaspoon ground coriander
1 teaspoon ground cumin
1 teaspoon ground turmeric
1 teaspoon sea salt
½ teaspoon ground ginger
Pepper to taste
1–13-ounce (400 ml) can coconut milk

Add all ingredients, except for the coconut milk to a large pot and bring to a boil. Reduce the heat and simmer for 30 minutes, stirring occasionally. In the final few minutes, add coconut milk, stirring until incorporated. Serve and enjoy!

SPINACH TOFU LASAGNA

The tofu beautifully replaces the cottage cheese or ricotta of a vegetarian lasagna and the spinach adds color, flavor and nutrients.

SERVES 8

- **1 box lasagna noodles (I use brown rice noodles)**
- **4 cups baby spinach**
- **2–23-ounce (700 ml) jars tomato pasta sauce**
- **1–14-ounce (400g) block firm tofu, drained**
- **2 cloves garlic, minced**
- **1 tablespoon low-sodium soy sauce or tamari**
- **2 tablespoons nutritional yeast**
- **1 cup dairy-free cheese shreds**

Preheat oven to 375°F.

Prepare lasagna noodles according to instructions on the box. In a bowl, mash tofu by hand and add soy sauce, minced garlic and nutritional yeast. Start with a bit of sauce in the bottom of a 9″ x 13″ or 22cm x 33cm rectangular deep baking dish, and then layer ⅓ of the noodles, ⅓ of the sauce, ½ of the tofu mixture, ½ of the spinach. Add another layer of noodles, sauce, tofu mixture, and spinach. For the final layer, add noodles topped with sauce, and then the dairy-free cheese.

Bake for 30 minutes uncovered and allow to cool for 10 minutes before serving.

FISHLESS FILLETS

A unique and tasty way to get to get some wonderful omega 3's into your body. These fillets are a favorite in our home, especially when served with Handmade Tartar Sauce (page 103).

SERVES 2-3

- **1–14-ounce (400g) block firm or extra firm tofu (not silken)**
- **1 sheet nori (roasted seaweed)**
- **2 tablespoons low-sodium soy sauce or tamari**
- **2 tablespoons flour (brown rice, spelt etc.)**
- **2 tablespoons nutritional yeast**
- **1 tablespoon organic corn meal**
- **¼ teaspoon sea salt**
- **¼ teaspoon dried dill**
- **1 tablespoon sunflower oil or coconut oil for pan-frying**

Cut the tofu block into eight evenly sized slices. Tear the nori sheet into four evenly sized squares. Place one piece of nori between two slices of tofu and repeat three more times until you have four fillets. They will look like tofu sandwiches with nori in the middle. You may have to fold the nori a little bit to have it fit between the tofu slices.

Create a light coating by mixing the flour, nutritional yeast, corn meal, sea salt, and dill in a medium sized bowl.

Place the soy sauce on a small plate and dip one fillet at a time in the liquid (on both sides), and then dip into the coating bowl until fully covered on both sides with the coating.

Heat the oil in a frying pan over medium heat and when hot, add the fillets. Pan fry for six to eight minutes on each side or until browned.

Serve with Handmade Tartar Sauce (page 103).

BIG BURRITO BOWL

My friends, Liberty and Chris are the geniuses behind this one. They created exceptional burritos in my kitchen recently and I watched them closely so I could convert what I saw into a big bowl recipe. There are so many wonderful flavors and textures to this, and topping it with the Cashew Sour Cream (page 97) makes it even more amazing.

SERVES 4

2 cups cooked quinoa or rice

BAKED ITEMS:

1 butternut squash, peeled and cubed

1–14-ounce (400g) block firm or extra firm tofu, cubed

2 tablespoons extra virgin olive oil

½ teaspoon cumin

¼ teaspoon sea salt

SAUTÉED ITEMS:

1 tablespoon coconut oil

½ white onion, finely chopped

1 zucchini, finely chopped

10 mushrooms, sliced

1 red pepper, thinly sliced

½ teaspoon ground cumin

½ teaspoon chili powder

Pinch of red pepper flakes

Pinch of sea salt

GARNISH:

2 cups salsa

1 cup fresh corn

Handful of fresh cilantro

2 avocados, sliced or cubed

Organic tortilla chips for garnishing edge of bowl

1 cup Cashew Sour Cream (page 97)

Preheat oven to 400°F.

Mix the cubed squash and tofu with the olive oil, cumin and pinch of sea salt in a bowl. Place on a baking sheet lined with parchment paper and bake for 30 minutes, stirring halfway through.

In a large frying pan over medium heat, add the coconut oil. Once it has melted, add the onion, zucchini, mushrooms, red pepper, spices, and salt. Sauté for approximately 10 minutes on medium-high heat, stirring often until the onions are soft and translucent. Cover and keep warm over low heat, until the baked items are ready.

To prepare each bowl, add ½ cup cooked quinoa or rice, a portion of squash and tofu, a portion of the sautéed veggies. Garnish with avocado, tortilla chips around the edges, fresh corn, salsa, and Cashew Sour Cream.

SHEPHERD'S SEED PIE

The perfect comfort food, this dish is always a crowd pleaser. Buckwheat (also called kasha) is the key to the amazing flavor of this dish. Buckwheat is actually a relative of rhubarb and despite its name, is a naturally gluten-free seed. Best smothered in a healthy serving of Nancy Zylstra's Gorgeous Gravy (page 98).

SERVES 8

SHEPHERD'S PIE:

- **2 cups tomato sauce**
- **1 cup water**
- **3 tablespoons low-sodium soy sauce**
- **2 carrots, thinly sliced**
- **2 cups cabbage, thinly sliced**
- **1 zucchini, sliced**
- **1 green pepper, finely chopped**
- **1 cup firm tofu, crumbled**
- **½ cup buckwheat kernels (groats)**
- **½ cup raw sunflower seeds, whole**
- **½ cup raw sunflower seeds, ground**
- **2 cloves garlic, minced**
- **½ teaspoon ground cumin**
- **Pepper to taste**

MASHED POTATO TOPPING:

- **6 large potatoes, chopped**
- **½-1 cup reserved potato water**
- **2 tablespoons Vegan Butter (page 104)**
- **½ teaspoon sea salt**

Preheat oven to 375°F.

Place all the shepherd's pie ingredients in a large pot, cover and bring to a boil. Reduce heat and simmer for 20 minutes.

Make the mashed potato topping by bringing a pot of water to a boil. Add the potatoes and cook until tender, about 15 minutes. When potatoes are cooked drain and reserve one cup of potato water. Slowly add up to ½ cup of potato water back into pot with the Vegan Butter and salt, and mash. If potatoes are not moist enough, add more reserved potato water until desired consistency is reached and set aside.

Spoon the cooked shepherd's pie contents into a large casserole dish and top with mashed potatoes. Bake uncovered for 40 minutes.

SPAGHETTI AND TOFU NEATBALLS

These neatballs are tasty little morsels. Make extra and throw them in your lunch for a wonderful surprise the next day!

SERVES 4-6

- **1 package spaghetti noodles (I use brown rice noodles)**
- **1 tablespoon ground or whole chia seeds**
- **3 tablespoons water**
- **1–14-ounce (400g) block of firm or extra firm tofu (not silken)**
- **½ yellow onion, minced**
- **5 mushrooms, minced**
- **2 tablespoons nutritional yeast**
- **1 teaspoon ground oregano**
- **1 teaspoon garlic powder**
- **½ teaspoon ground thyme**
- **1–23-ounce (700 ml) jar tomato pasta sauce**
- **½ cup of Vegan Parmesan** **(see page 105)**

Preheat oven to 400°F.

Create a "chia egg" by combining the chia seeds with the water in a small bowl. Stir and set aside.

Hand crumble the tofu in a large bowl and mix with onion, mushrooms, nutritional yeast, oregano, garlic, thyme, and the "chia egg". Using your hands form small "neatballs" and place them on a parchment paper covered baking sheet. Bake for 25 minutes or until nice and brown. While neatballs are baking, cook the spaghetti according to package directions and warm up the pasta sauce in a saucepan on the stove.

Serve the cooked spaghetti in individual bowls topped with sauce and "neatballs" and then more sauce. Sprinkle Vegan Parmesan on top.

CREAMY MAC AND CHEESE

Mac and Cheese is about as comfort food as it gets. This might be the creamiest mac and cheese out there, and as a bonus it is full of nutrient dense veggies!

SERVES 4-6

1 medium sweet potato, peeled and cubed

2 cups butternut squash, peeled and cubed

2 carrots, chopped

½ of 13-ounce (400 ml) can full fat coconut milk*

¼ cup nutritional yeast

1 tablespoon miso paste

½ teaspoon prepared mustard

½ teaspoon sea salt

Pepper to taste

1 pound (454 grams) brown rice macaroni noodles

Place sweet potato, squash and carrots in a medium sized pot and cover with water. Cover the pot with lid and bring the water to a boil. Reduce the heat to a simmer and cook until the veggies are soft (about 12-15 minutes). Once the veggies are cooked, drain and place them in a blender with the coconut milk, nutritional yeast, miso, mustard, and salt. Blend until smooth. Cook the pasta according to the package directions. Once the pasta is cooked and drained, return it to the pot and stir in the cheesy sauce. Add pepper to taste and serve.

* *Typically when you open a can of coconut milk, the cream and water have separated. Pour the contents of the can into a deep bowl and mix together, then use half of the mixture in this recipe.*

ARTICHOKE, RED PEPPER & KALE PIZZA

This pizza looks almost like a deep dish with the layers of plump artichokes, veggies and gooey, dairy-free cheese.

MAKES 1 PIZZA THAT SERVES 2-3

- **1 prepared pizza crust**
- **¼-½ cup of pizza sauce (depending on how saucy you like it)**
- **1 cup dairy-free mozzarella shreds**
- **1–14-ounce (398ml) can artichokes, drained, rinsed and chopped**
- **1 red pepper, thinly sliced**
- **½ cup black olives, sliced**
- **½ cup de-stemmed kale, finely chopped**

Preheat oven to 375°F.

Add sauce to pizza crust and then add a layer of half of the veggies (artichokes, kale, red peppers, and olives). Sprinkle half of the cheese, and then add the remaining veggies and top with the remaining cheese.

Bake for 10-12 minutes or until the cheese has started melting. Remove from the oven and allow the pizza to sit for five minutes before slicing.

ROASTED VEGGIE PESTO PIZZA

My partner attended a retreat a few years ago and came home describing a pizza made with roasted beets and pesto that she absolutely loved. I thought it sounded amazing, and after a few attempts, she says I've managed to nail it!

MAKES 1 PIZZA THAT SERVES 2-3

TIP

When I use organic beets and sweet potatoes I don't bother peeling them as the skin is incredibly nutrient dense. Just give them a good wash and they are ready to chop.

ROASTED VEGGIES:

- **2 medium beets, chopped into cubes**
- **1 sweet potato, chopped into cubes**
- **1 cup firm tofu, chopped into cubes**
- **1 tablespoon extra virgin olive oil**

Pinch of sea salt

PESTO:

- **1 cup fresh basil**
- **¼ cup extra virgin olive oil**
- **¼ cup raw cashews**
- **3 cloves garlic, minced**
- **¼ cup nutritional yeast**
- **½ teaspoon sea salt**
- **½ teaspoon black pepper**

REMAINING INGREDIENTS:

- **1 prepared pizza crust**
- **1 cup cherry tomatoes, cut in half**

Preheat oven to 375°F.

Place chopped beets, tofu and sweet potatoes in a bowl and add olive oil and salt. Stir until coated. Place on a baking sheet lined with parchment paper and bake uncovered for 35 minutes, stirring once at the halfway point until vegetables are tender and getting roasted edges.

Place pesto ingredients in a blender or food processor and blend until you have a smooth texture. Spread pesto onto prepared pizza crust. When the roasted veggies are ready, place them in a bowl and mix in the cherry tomatoes. Add veggies on top of the pesto covered crust and bake the pizza for 10 minutes.

TEMPEH COCONUT STIR FRY

Tempeh is a nice alternative to tofu because it is fermented first and easier to digest. It is also extremely high in protein and has a nice chewy texture. The combination of the tanginess of tempeh with the creaminess of coconut milk feels truly decadent. Serve over rice or quinoa with a nice side salad for a wonderful meal.

SERVES 4

2 tablespoons water

½ large white or yellow onion, diced

1–8-ounce (225g) package tempeh, cut into thin slices

1 red pepper, sliced thinly

1 orange, green or yellow pepper, sliced thinly

1 cup red cabbage, sliced thinly

6 mushrooms, sliced

2 tablespoons low-sodium soy sauce

1 clove garlic, minced

1 teaspoon ground turmeric

1 teaspoon ground cumin

½ teaspoon ground coriander

1–13-ounce (400 ml) can full fat coconut milk

Heat a frying pan over medium-high heat and add the water and onions. Sauté the onions for five minutes before adding the remaining ingredients (except for the coconut milk). Sauté for 10 minutes and then add the coconut milk. Continue cooking for a couple of minutes and serve.

STUFFED TOFU ROAST

This is the ultimate holiday centerpiece, and so much better than anything you can buy in a box. I have been making this for many years on special occasions, and even my non-veg friends and family love this meal. Make it extra special with Nancy Zylstra's Gorgeous Gravy (page 98) poured over each slice.

SERVES 8-10

TOFU ROAST:

- **4–14-ounce (400g) blocks firm or extra firm tofu (do not use silken tofu)**
- **3 tablespoons tamari**
- **2 teaspoons dried sage or poultry seasoning**

SAVORY STUFFING (see page 119)

BASTING SAUCE:

- **¼ cup toasted sesame oil**
- **¼ cup tamari**
- **2 tablespoons orange juice concentrate**
- **1 teaspoon ground pepper**

Mix all ingredients together in a small bowl.

Preheat oven to 375°F.

Place the tofu, three tablespoons tamari and the sage or poultry seasoning in a large bowl and crumble the tofu by hand until it is very fine and all the lumps are gone.

Line an average-sized colander with cheese cloth. Transfer crumbled tofu into the colander and press it down firmly with your hands, paying special attention to the edges, making sure it is all firmly pressed into the colander with all excess moisture squeezed out.

Using a spoon, dig out the center of the tofu to create space for the stuffing. Place the tofu you have removed into a bowl and set it aside. Dig out tofu so there is still at least one inch of tofu left in the colander on all sides. Fill this space with the savory stuffing. Next, create the tofu roast base by using the tofu that has been set aside. Simply add it as a "top layer" to seal in the stuffing. Spread evenly and press down firmly. This will be the bottom of the roast once flipped over in the next step.

Line a cookie sheet with parchment paper and carefully turn the colander onto the cookie sheet so that you have what looks like a tofu dome on the sheet. Then, baste it with the basting sauce. Bake for one hour, basting again halfway through the baking process.

MAPLE GLAZED TOFU

This is part of what we call "the standard" dinner in my home. Standard because it ends up on our plates at least once a week. So simple, and yet so tasty. We usually enjoy this dish combined with roasted potato wedges and steamed broccoli. There is no need to marinade the tofu ahead of time, as the sauce incorporates beautifully as the tofu cooks.

SERVES 2-3

- **1–14-ounce (400g) block of firm or extra firm tofu (not silken or boxed tofu)**
- **3 tablespoons low-sodium soy sauce**
- **2 tablespoons maple syrup**
- **2 cloves garlic, minced**
- **1 tablespoon rice vinegar**
- **1 tablespoon fresh minced ginger or ½ teaspoon ground ginger**

In a medium sized bowl, mix together the soy sauce, maple syrup, garlic, vinegar, and ginger. Pour into a large frying pan over medium heat. Slice the tofu into thin slices or triangles and add to the pan. Cook for eight to ten minutes, flipping halfway through.

TIP

Try experimenting with different vinegars with this recipe. It is wonderful with balsamic, apple cider or red wine vinegar.

CHICKPEA QUINOA BURGERS

Homemade burgers on the grill with lots of delicious flavors. The great texture comes from using shredded zucchini so that the burgers stay moist when they cook.

MAKES 7 BURGERS

2 cups cooked chickpeas
1 cup cooked quinoa
¾ cup shredded zucchini
2 cloves garlic, minced
2 green onions, minced
1 carrot, minced
½ white onion, minced
½ cup brown rice or oat flour
Handful of cilantro, chopped
1 teaspoon hot sauce (optional)
1 teaspoon mustard
½ teaspoon sea salt
Pepper to taste

Place chickpeas in a bowl and mash with a potato masher until mostly mashed, but with some chunks remaining. Add in remaining ingredients and stir well (using hands is best). Form burgers by taking ½ cup of the mixture at a time and forming a tight ball in your hands. Flatten so burgers remain somewhat thick. Barbecue on low-medium heat, flipping after a few minutes. Press down with spatula and grill other side.

VARIATION

Oven baked burgers: Preheat oven to 400°F and bake for 25-30 minutes on a baking sheet lined with parchment paper.

****SEE PHOTO ON FRONT COVER.****

TEMPEH SLOPPY JOES

The grown-up version of one of my childhood favorites. This is a neat way to get more tempeh into your life. Take your time crumbling the tempeh so it ends up looking ground.

SERVES 3-4

1 tablespoon coconut oil
1 medium onion, chopped
1 clove garlic, minced
1–8-ounce (225g) package tempeh, crumbled by hand
2 tablespoons low-sodium soy sauce
2 cups tomato sauce
¾ cup water
½ cup white basmati rice
½ tablespoon chili powder
1 tablespoon maple syrup
½ teaspoon black pepper
Whole grain buns

In a large saucepan over medium heat, add the oil, onions and garlic. Cook until the onions have softened. Add the crumbled tempeh, rice, soy sauce, tomato sauce, water, chili powder, maple syrup, and pepper. Bring to a simmer and cook for 15-20 minutes on medium-low heat or until rice is soft.

Stir occasionally to prevent sticking. Once cooked serve over whole grain buns.

ORANGE SESAME GLAZED TEMPEH

The tangy orange glaze is slightly sweet and gingery and compliments the natural nuttiness of the tempeh.

SERVES 3-4

- 1–8-ounce (225g) package tempeh
- 2 tablespoons concentrated frozen orange juice
- 2 tablespoons sesame seeds
- 2 cloves garlic, minced
- 1 tablespoon tamari (or low-sodium soy sauce)
- 1 tablespoon toasted sesame oil
- ½ teaspoon ground ginger
- Pepper to taste

Create the marinade by combining the orange juice concentrate, sesame seeds, garlic, tamari, toasted sesame oil, ginger, and pepper in a bowl, stirring to combine.

Heat a frying pan to medium heat. Cut the tempeh into thin triangles and place in the frying pan. Immediately pour marinade over tempeh and cook eight to ten minutes on each side or until it begins to brown.

BLACK BEAN TACOS

Quick, colourful and hearty, these tasty tacos are best when served with Cashew Sour Cream (page 97).

SERVES 3-4

8 soft tortillas (corn or wheat)

2 avocados, cut into small cubes

2 tomatoes, chopped

2 cups salsa (divided)

Handful of cilantro, chopped

1 lime, cut into 8 slices

1–13-ounce (398 ml) can of black beans, drained and rinsed

1 cup Cashew Sour Cream (see page 97)

Heat the beans in a medium sized sauce pan with ½ cup of the salsa over medium-to-low heat until warm; set aside. Warm tortillas according to package directions. In each warm tortilla, place a heaping spoonful of each of the warm beans, avocado, salsa and tomato. Squirt some fresh lime juice on top, and then finish it with a healthy dollop of Cashew Sour Cream and a sprinkle of fresh cilantro.

Maple Pecan Coconut Ice Cream (page 169)

Chapter 9

DESSERTS

SHAKE IT UP COCONUT WHIPPED CREAM

Easy, dreamy coconut whipped cream that does not require an electric mixer. All you need is a mason jar with a lid and a couple of strong arms for shaking the cream into whipped cream. Serve on top of desserts or milkshakes for that extra special touch.

MAKES 1 CUP

1–13-ounce (400 ml) can full-fat coconut milk *Chilled*
1 tablespoon maple syrup
¼ teaspoon pure vanilla extract

Chill the can of coconut milk in the fridge for about four hours so the cream rises to the top. Open can and remove the coconut cream carefully leaving the coconut water behind. Use the coconut water in your next smoothie.

Place the coconut cream in a mason jar and add the maple syrup and vanilla extract. Tighten the lid firmly and shake the jar vigorously for three to four minutes, or until the cream is thick and fluffy. Serve immediately, or place in the fridge where it will continue to thicken.

NOTE: If you have an electric hand mixer or a stand mixer with the whisk attachment you can use it to beat the whipped cream.
Beat on high speed until fluffy (five to seven minutes).

NUTTY CARAMEL APPLES

Kids love this healthier version of a caramel apple, and as I found out in one of my cooking classes, adults go kind of crazy for them too.

MAKES 9 CARAMEL APPLES

9 apples (any variety)
1 cup dates, pitted
6 tablespoons maple syrup
6 tablespoons melted coconut oil
2 teaspoons pure vanilla extract
Pinch of sea salt
1 cup chopped nuts (e.g. almonds, pecans or walnuts)
9 popsicle sticks

Place the dates, maple syrup, melted coconut oil, vanilla, and salt in a blender and blend until smooth. (If your blender is less powerful, soak the dates for one hour in hot water and then drain before you blend). Insert a popsicle stick about halfway into each apple and then spoon on the caramel coating. Sprinkle with chopped nuts and place in the fridge. Allow to chill for 30 minutes and serve.

1 TEASPOON
(5.0 ML)

LEMON BLUEBERRY CAKE

Lemon and blueberries are the perfect, tangy combination. They are beautiful in this simple, yet scrumptious cake. There is no need to ice this cake, just add more blueberries on top, and serve.

SERVES 6

- **1½ cups flour (oat, spelt, all purpose, etc.)**
- **1½ teaspoons baking powder**
- **½ teaspoon baking soda**
- **½ teaspoon ground cinnamon**
- **¼ teaspoon sea salt**
- **1 cup plant milk (soy, almond, cashew etc.)**
- **⅔ cup sugar**
- **2 tablespoons coconut oil, just melted**
- **1 teaspoon lemon zest**
- **1 teaspoon pure vanilla extract**
- **1½ cups frozen or fresh blueberries + ½ cup more for topping**

Preheat oven to 350°F.

Mix the flour, baking powder, baking soda, cinnamon, and salt in a large bowl, and set aside. In a medium-size bowl, mix together the plant milk, sugar, coconut oil, lemon zest, and vanilla. Pour the wet ingredients into the bowl with the dry ingredients, mixing gently. Add the blueberries and stir. Pour the cake batter into a 11″ x 7″ cake pan, oiled or lined with parchment paper. Bake for 30-35 minutes or until the edges of the cake are browned. Allow the cake to cool and top it with additional blueberries when serving.

CARROT CAKE WITH CREAM CHEESE ICING

I created this cake to celebrate my sweetie's birthday a couple of years ago. Imagine a moist and spicy carrot cake topped with a velvety cream cheese icing, all made from plants. If you are just getting started with vegan baking, this a great cake to try. You will see how moist vegan baking can be, and how chia/ flax eggs work well to bind the cake together.

SERVES 8

DRY INGREDIENTS:

- **2½ cups all-purpose flour**
- **1 teaspoon baking soda**
- **1 teaspoon ground cinnamon**
- **½ teaspoon ground nutmeg**
- **½ teaspoon sea salt**

EGG-LIKE BINDER:

- **3 tablespoons ground flax or whole or ground chia seeds**
- **½ cup water**

WET INGREDIENTS:

- **1¼ cups sugar**
- **½ cup unsweetened applesauce**
- **½ cup crushed pineapple**
- **½ cup sunflower oil or melted coconut oil**
- **1 teaspoon pure vanilla extract**
- **2 cups finely shredded carrots**
- **1 cup walnuts + ¼ cup more to sprinkle on top**

CREAM CHEESE ICING:

- **8 ounces (227g) vegan cream cheese**
- **1 cup powdered sugar**
- **¼ cup Vegan Butter (page 104) or slightly melted coconut oil**
- **1 teaspoon pure vanilla extract**

Preheat oven to 350°F and line a 9″×11″ baking pan with parchment paper.

Gather up large, medium and small bowls. Mix dry ingredients in a large bowl and set aside. Mix the egg-like binder in a small bowl and set aside. Mix the wet ingredients in a medium-size bowl. When the wet ingredients are well mixed, add into the large bowl with the dry ingredients. Add the egg-like binder to the large bowl as well, and mix everything until well combined. Spoon the batter into the prepared baking pan and bake 30-35 minutes or until a toothpick comes out clean when inserted into the center of the cake.

Make the icing by combining all the icing ingredients in a bowl and mixing until icing is very smooth. When cake has cooled, ice the cake and sprinkle remaining walnuts on top and around the edges.

CHOCOLATE CAKE WITH VELVETY GANACHE

This is a fluffy, foolproof delicious chocolate cake topped with a velvety and extremely satisfying ganache. Ganache is so much better than traditional frosting because you can skip the icing sugar and butter and just use the cream from a can of coconut milk.

SERVES 8

- **1½ cups all-purpose flour**
- **¼ cup cocoa powder**
- **1 teaspoon baking soda**
- **1 teaspoon baking powder**
- **½ teaspoon sea salt**
- **¾ cup sugar**
- **1 cup cold plant milk (cashew, rice, almond etc.)**
- **1 tablespoon apple cider vinegar**
- **4 tablespoons sunflower oil or safflower oil**
- **1 teaspoon pure vanilla extract**

GANACHE

- **½ - ⅔ cup coconut cream from a 13-ounce (400 ml) can of full fat coconut milk**
- **½ - ⅔ cup dairy free chocolate chips**
- **2 tablespoons maple syrup**
- **½ teaspoon pure vanilla extract**

Refrigerate the can of coconut milk for at least three hours (or overnight) so cream rises to the top inside the can.

Preheat oven to 350°F.

In a large bowl, whisk the plant milk and vinegar together and allow to sit for five minutes to activate. Next, add the oil, vanilla extract, flour, cocoa, baking soda, baking powder, and salt to the bowl, stirring the ingredients together until well mixed. This recipe uses a minimal amount of sugar, so at this point, taste for sweetness and add up to ¼ cup more sugar if desired.

Pour the batter into a 9" x 11" rectangular pan lined with parchment paper, and bake for 40-45 minutes or until a toothpick inserted into the center, comes out clean. Allow the cake to cool completely before adding the ganache.

GANACHE

Carefully open the can of coconut milk and remove the firm cream at the top of the can, leaving the coconut water behind (use the coconut water in your next smoothie). Use ½ cup of the cream for a regular amount of icing and ⅔ cup for extra icing, or if you are choosing to cut the cake into halves, icing between the two layers.

Place the coconut cream into a small saucepan and heat over medium heat until almost at a boil. While it is warming, add an equivalent amount of chocolate chips to a medium-size bowl and set aside. (i.e. if you are using ½ cup coconut cream, use ½ cup chocolate chips).

When the coconut cream has almost boiled remove it from the stove and pour it over the waiting chocolate chips. Add the maple syrup and vanilla to the mixture, leaving it for five minutes while the chocolate begins to melt. After five minutes, gently stir everything together until you have a shiny chocolate ganache. Allow the ganache to cool for 30 minutes before icing your cake with it.

VARIATION

After Eight Cake: Turn the ganache into chocolate mint with just one change. Replace the vanilla extract with ½ teaspoon peppermint extract.

CHOCOLATE TOFU CHEESECAKE

This was one of the first vegan recipes I ever attempted. It was a winner right from the start and I have made this countless times for people who love it and never suspect the main ingredient is tofu.

SERVES 10

CRUST:

1 cup big fresh dates (e.g. Medjool), pitted

1 cup whole raw almonds (or 1 cup almond meal)

¼ cup cocoa powder

1 tablespoon coconut oil, melted + a bit more for the pie plate

½ teaspoon sea salt

CHEESECAKE:

15-ounces (450g) soft or silken tofu

½ cup sugar

1 cup dairy-free chocolate chips

½ teaspoon pure vanilla extract

Pinch of sea salt

Preheat oven to 350°F.

Prepare a 10 inch pie plate by oiling it with melted coconut oil, or by lining it with parchment paper. To make the crust, pit the dates and soak them in a bowl covered with hot water for 10 minutes. Drain, and set aside. If using whole almonds, place the almonds into a blender or food processor and process them until you have a finely ground texture, without any large pieces. Remove the ground almonds from the blender, placing them into a medium-size bowl. Next, place the dates, cocoa, melted coconut oil, and salt in the blender or food processor, and process until you have date paste. Mix the date paste into the almond meal or ground almonds (by hand is best), and then with moist hands press the mixture into the oiled pie plate. Press firmly along the base and the edges.

Melt the chocolate chips in a small pot over low heat carefully—don't let them burn. Alternatively, you can use a double boiler. Once the chocolate chips are melted, add the melted chocolate, tofu, sugar, vanilla, and salt into a blender. Blend together until very smooth.

Pour into pie crust and bake 40 minutes. Allow to cool and then refrigerate for two hours before serving.

FUDGY BLACK BEAN BROWNIES

This is a truly remarkable recipe because it does not use oil, sugar, butter, or eggs and you still get wickedly delicious brownies. Your dinner guests will have no idea they are eating protein-rich black beans for dessert! The trick is in the black beans replacing the eggs and oil, and the dates replacing the sugar. There is an option to add in non-dairy chocolate chips, which I highly recommend if you are looking for a richer chocolate experience.

SERVES 8

- **2 cups big fresh dates (e.g. Medjool, pitted)**
- **1–15-ounce (440 ml) can of black beans, rinsed and drained**
- **1½ teaspoons pure vanilla extract**
- **¾ cup oat flour (grind rolled oats in blender or coffee grinder)**
- **½ cup cocoa powder**
- **1 tablespoon ground flax seeds**
- **1 teaspoon baking powder**
- **½ teaspoon baking soda**
- **½ teaspoon sea salt**
- **½ cup non-dairy chocolate chips (optional)**
- **½ cup chopped pecans or walnuts**

Preheat the oven to 350°F.

First turn the dates into date paste by placing the dates in a bowl and covering with hot water, using just enough water to cover the dates. In about five minutes the dates will appear flaky and swollen. At this point pour off the water, reserving ½ cup of the soaking water. Blend the reserved soaking water with the dates and the vanilla extract in a blender or food processor until smooth. Next add the black beans and blend together until smooth and then spoon out mixture into a large bowl.

In a separate medium sized bowl, mix the flour, cocoa powder, ground flaxseeds, baking powder, baking soda, and sea salt. Now transfer these dry ingredients into the bowl with the date and bean mixture. Stir in the nuts and chocolate chips until well mixed.

Spoon the batter into an 8″ x 8″ baking pan lined with parchment paper, and spread until smooth. Bake for 25-30 minutes. Allow to cool before serving.

CHOCOLATE DREAM BARS

Imagine melty chocolate, gooey caramel sauce, coconut, and nuts all in an easy-to-grab square of delight. These are what sweet vegan dreams are made of.

MAKES ABOUT 12 SQUARES

CARAMEL SAUCE:

2 cups vanilla soy or cashew milk (you can use other plant milks but these work best)

⅓ cup sugar

Pinch sea salt

1 teaspoon pure vanilla extract

GRAHAM CRACKER CRUST:

1½ cups graham cracker crumbs

Few pinches sea salt

2½ tablespoons maple syrup

2 tablespoons melted coconut oil

DREAMY TOPPING:

¾ cup unsweetened shredded coconut

1 cup dairy free chocolate chips

½ cup finely chopped walnuts or pecans

Preheat oven to 350°F.

To make the caramel sauce, bring the plant milk, sugar and salt to a boil in a medium sized pot with no lid, and then reduce the heat to a simmer. Simmer for 30 minutes to reduce the caramel sauce down, stirring occasionally. You will know it is ready when it is reduced to one cup. At this point, remove the mixture from the stove and stir in vanilla extract.

While the caramel sauce is cooking, prepare the graham cracker crust by mixing the graham cracker crumbs together with the salt, maple syrup and melted oil in a large bowl. Press into a lightly oiled or parchment-paper-lined 8″ x 8″ pan.

When the sauce is ready, spoon onto graham cracker crust and then sprinkle the coconut, chocolate chips and nuts on top. Bake for 20-25 minutes or until caramel is bubbling up in spots and coconut is turning golden brown. Allow to cool and cut into squares.

REGGIE'S DATE SQUARES

Dedicated to my dad, Reggie. My dad loved date squares so much that the date square recipe page in the Purity cookbook I grew up with, was completely worn out. This is my vegan version. I know he would have loved these.

MAKES 12 DATE SQUARES

1 cup chopped dates

½ cup water

2 cups rolled oats

1 cup oat flour*

½ cup Vegan Butter (page 104) or melted coconut oil

½ cup brown sugar

½ teaspoon baking soda

¼ teaspoon sea salt

Preheat the oven to 350°F.

Place the chopped dates and water in small pot and bring to a boil over medium-high heat. Reduce heat and simmer for five minutes, stirring often. Remove from stove and allow to cool.

In a large bowl, mix the rolled oats, oat flour, baking soda, and sea salt.

In a small bowl, mix together the Vegan Butter and sugar. Add the butter and sugar mixture to the oat mixture and combine well, using your hands to really create a nice, sticky mixture.

Press half of the mixture into an 8" x 8" pan lined with parchment paper or slightly oiled to form the base; then, spread the cooked dates onto the base. Cover the dates with the remaining oat mixture, firmly pressing to completely cover the dates.

Bake 20-25 minutes.

* *To make oat flour simply grind rolled oats in a coffee grinder, food processor or blender.*

CHOCOLATE CHIP COOKIE ICE CREAM SANDWICHES

Imagine delicious vegan ice cream sandwiches coming out of your freezer. It's more than possible, and this recipe is quite simple, it just takes a little more time because of all of the freezing required between steps. I promise that you won't regret your time investment!

MAKES 5 ICE CREAM SANDWICHES

COOKIE DRY INGREDIENTS:

1⅓ cups oat flour, spelt flour or all-purpose flour

½ teaspoon baking soda

½ teaspoon sea salt

COOKIE WET INGREDIENTS:

1 chia or flax egg*

⅓ cup sunflower or safflower oil

½ cup sugar

½ cup dairy free chocolate chips

½ teaspoon pure vanilla extract

Preheat the oven to 350°F.

* *Make one "chia or flax egg" by combining one tablespoon ground chia or flax seeds with three tablespoons water in a small bowl. Let the mixture sit for 10 minutes or until mix becomes gelatinous.*

In a large bowl, add the dry ingredients: flour, baking soda and salt; stir until well mixed. In a smaller bowl, combine the wet ingredients: oil, vanilla, sugar, and chia or flax egg; stir until well combined.

Add the wet ingredients from the small bowl into the dry ingredients in the large bowl and stir until well mixed. Add the chocolate chips and mix in until well combined.

NOTE: if needed, you can add one tablespoon of extra water to help the cookie dough ingredients stick together.

Use approximately two tablespoons of the cookie dough at a time to create a ball, then press each ball onto a baking sheet. Bake for 12-14 minutes or until the cookies begin to brown.

See Vanilla Coconut Ice Cream recipe on next page for final steps (see small photo shown on back cover).

VANILLA COCONUT ICE CREAM

Great on its own and even more so as the filling for the Chocolate Chip Cookie Ice Cream Sandwiches recipe.

SERVES 2-3

1–13-ounce (400 ml) can full-fat coconut milk *Chilled*

¼ cup maple syrup

½ teaspoon pure vanilla extract

Refrigerate the can of coconut milk for at least three hours, or overnight so the cream rises to the top of the can. Open the coconut milk carefully and remove the firm cream at the top of the can, leaving the coconut water behind (use the coconut water in your next smoothie).

Place the coconut cream, maple syrup and vanilla in a blender; blend until just smooth. Spoon the mixture into a medium-sized bowl and freeze it for at least two hours.

IF USING TO FILL ICE CREAM SANDWICHES:

Remove the ice cream from the freezer and allow it to thaw for about 20 minutes, so that it becomes soft enough to spread. Take two cookies and spread about ⅕ of the ice cream on the bottom of one cookie, pressing the second cookie into the ice cream to form a sandwich.

Repeat this process until you have five ice cream sandwiches. Return them to the freezer for at least one hour so that the ice cream sandwiches are nice and solid.

Makes 5 ice cream sandwiches

CHOCOLATE PEANUT BUTTER ICE CREAM

Insanely delicious, creamy, decadent and totally plant-based! This might be your "go-to" the treat of the summer!

SERVES 2-3

1–13-ounce (400 ml) can full-fat coconut milk *Chilled*

¼ cup maple syrup

2 tablespoons natural peanut butter

2½ tablespoons cocoa or raw cacao powder

½ teaspoon pure vanilla extract

A few cacao nibs to sprinkle on top (optional)

Chill the can of coconut milk in the fridge for about four hours so the cream rises to the top. Open can and remove the coconut cream carefully leaving the coconut water behind.

Add the coconut cream, maple syrup, peanut butter, cocoa or cacao powder, and vanilla extract to a blender. Blend until just smooth and pour into two or three small bowls or ice cream dishes. If you have cacao nibs sprinkle them on top. Place in the freezer for two hours until the ice cream is solid. Remove the desserts from freezer, allowing them to soften for about 20 minutes before serving.

MAPLE PECAN COCONUT MILK ICE CREAM

Although soy, almond, coconut, and cashew ice cream pints are wonderful, you may never again go back to the store-bought version with this simple creamy and delicious recipe at your fingertips.

SERVES 2-3

1–13-ounce (400 ml) can full fat coconut milk *Chilled*

¼ cup maple syrup

1 teaspoon pure vanilla extract

2 tablespoons pecans, finely chopped

Pinch of sea salt

Chill the can of coconut milk in the fridge for about four hours so the cream rises to the top. Open the can and remove the coconut cream, carefully leaving the coconut water behind.

Place the coconut cream, maple syrup, vanilla, and sea salt in a blender or food processor and blend until just smooth. Be careful not to over-blend or the texture will become chunky. Once smooth, add the pecans and blend slightly until the pecans are incorporated. Spoon into three small bowls and let freeze for two hours. Remove from the freezer allowing to thaw slightly before serving.

****SEE PHOTO ON PAGE 150.****

HANDMADE CHOCOLATE TURTLES

I loved diving into a box of turtle chocolates at Christmas when I was growing up. The memory of the combination of caramel, pecans and chocolate inspired me to create something not only vegan, but healthier. These turtles are a lot of fun to make, perhaps, the most fun you will have in the kitchen all year.

MAKES 30 CHOCOLATES

12 soft fresh dates (e.g. Medjool), pitted (about 1 cup)

1 tablespoon pure vanilla extract

Pinch of sea salt

¾ cup dairy free chocolate (semi-sweet chocolate chips or a couple of dark chocolate bars work well)

1 cup whole pecans

Place the dates, vanilla and sea salt in a bowl. Mix them together with your hands for a few minutes, until the dates are soft and the vanilla has been absorbed. Form 30 small balls about the size of a large marble, and then slightly flatten them. These will be your caramel centers. Cut half of the pecans lengthwise to form the legs, sticking one end of each of them into the caramel center. Use another small piece of pecan for the turtle head and a small piece for the tail.

Melt the chocolate in a double boiler, or very carefully in a small pot over low heat, stirring continuously so that the chocolate does not burn. Once melted, remove the melted chocolate from heat. Place a smaller dab of melted chocolate on the bottom of the turtle. This will help hold the legs in place. Then, place the turtle, bottom side down on a sheet of parchment paper. Put a nice dab of chocolate to cover the top of the turtle. Once all the turtles are formed, place in the fridge to set.

OATMEAL CHOCOLATE CHIP COOKIES

These cookies are so chocolatey, so chewy and totally filled with the goodness of oats. I make these at least once a week in our home. They are always a huge hit.

MAKES 10 COOKIES

TIP

Eggs have traditionally been used in baking to bind ingredients together. Chia Eggs are a much better way to keep everything from falling apart. Chia seeds are a superfood and their health benefits are a mile long. Not only do they have the omega 3's, which our bodies crave, they are also rich in health-promoting fiber. Next time you are making cookies, muffins or cake replace your eggs with Chia Eggs for perfect, nutrient-dense results.

DRY INGREDIENTS:

1⅓ cups oat flour

½ cup rolled oats

½ teaspoon baking soda

½ teaspoon sea salt

WET INGREDIENTS:

1 chia or flax egg*

⅓ cup sunflower or safflower oil

½ cup sugar

½ cup dairy free chocolate chips

½ teaspoon pure vanilla extract

Preheat the oven to 350°F.

* *Make one chia or flax egg by combining one tablespoon ground chia or flax seeds with three tablespoons water, using a small whisk, in a small bowl. Let the mixture sit for 10 minutes, or until the mix becomes gelatinous.*

In a large bowl, add the dry ingredients: flour, oats, baking soda, and salt. Stir until well mixed. In a smaller bowl, combine the wet ingredients: oil, sugar, vanilla, and chia or flax egg, stirring until well combined.

Add the wet ingredients from the small bowl into the dry ingredients of the large bowl and stir until well mixed. Add the chocolate chips and mix until well combined.

NOTE: you can add one tablespoon of extra water to help the cookie dough become stickier if it is still quite dry.

Using approximately one to two tablespoons of the cookie dough at a time, roll the mixture into a ball, and then press it onto a baking sheet. Bake for 12-14 minutes or until they begin to brown.

PERFECT PECAN PIE

When I was young, pecan pie was the ultimate treat. Creating a vegan version was a lot of fun. This pie is filled with all the best qualities of a pecan pie: sticky, sweet, nutty, and oh so delicious.

SERVES 8

BASE:

1 cup whole shelled pecans

1 cup unsweetened shredded coconut

2 tablespoons melted coconut oil + a bit more for the pie plate

6 big fresh dates, pitted

Pinch of sea salt

PIE:

1 cup maple syrup

1 cup coconut or soy creamer

1 cup whole shelled pecans

¼ cup brown rice flour

Preheat oven to 375°F.

To make the base, place the pecans, coconut, melted coconut oil, dates, and salt together in a blender or food processor. Blend or process until no longer chunky, and somewhat sticky. Prepare a pie plate by oiling liberally with extra melted coconut oil. Press base ingredients firmly into pie plate and bake 10-14 minutes.

Mix the maple syrup, creamer, and flour in a bowl, until smooth. Add the pecans and stir a few times. Pour the mix into the baked pie shell. Bake 35-40 minutes and allow to cool before placing in the refrigerator to set for two hours.

TIP

You can find the coconut or soy creamer in the dairy cooler of your grocery store with other coffee creamers.

Francis
Dharma
Zoey

Chapter 10

DOGGIE TREATS

CHEESY DOG COOKIES

Mostly these are for dogs, however hungry dog walkers enjoy them too! These cookies have saved my partner on numerous dog walks when she had not eaten enough before leaving home. Just be sure that if you choose to imbibe, that you are willing to generously share. Our dogs are very good at keeping track of these cookies!

MAKES ABOUT 50 COOKIES

3 cups flour (oat, spelt etc.)
2 tablespoons ground flax seeds
½ cup water
⅓ cup nutritional yeast
¼ cup natural peanut butter
2 tablespoon extra virgin olive oil or melted coconut oil

Preheat oven to 375°F.

Create two flax eggs by mixing water and ground flax in a small bowl. Set aside for 10 minutes to thicken. Mix the flour and nutritional yeast in a large bowl. In a medium-size bowl, mix the peanut butter and oil, adding in the flax eggs and combining well. Now pour the wet ingredients into the bowl with the dry ingredients, mixing until you have a nice cookie dough consistency.

Roll the dough out onto a countertop that has been sprinkled with more flour, or onto parchment paper. Flatten the dough with a rolling pin. Use a cookie cutter to make fun cookie shapes.

Bake 20-25 minutes or until they begin to brown.

THANKSGIVING DOG COOKIES

These smell like a wonderful vegan thanksgiving meal when they are baking in the oven. Our dog, Francis sits by the oven door, occasionally pawing at it every time I make them.

MAKES ABOUT 25 COOKIES

1 cup flour (oat, spelt etc.)
¾ cup rolled oats
1 teaspoon poultry seasoning (or a blend of sage and thyme)
1 teaspoon garlic powder
½ cup coconut oil, melted
water as needed

Preheat oven to 375°F.

Mix the flour and rolled oats in a large bowl with the garlic powder and poultry seasoning. Stir in the coconut oil, mixing until you have a nice cookie dough consistency. If the mix is still dry, add water, one tablespoon at a time.

Roll the dough out onto countertop that has been sprinkled with more flour, or onto parchment paper. Flatten the dough with a rolling pin. Use a cookie cutter to make fun cookie shapes.

Bake 20-25 minutes or until they begin to brown.

WOOFEY BITES

Think of these as bliss bites for dogs. Just like people bliss bites, these don't need to be baked. Our dogs love these so much, they lay on the floor by my feet when I am making them. Don't let your furry pal fool you into thinking she/he should eat the whole batch at once; these are high calorie treats and just a couple of them go a long way. They are easy to pack and make a perfect snack on a long hike.

MAKES ABOUT 50 WOOFEY BITES

BLEND INTO A FLOUR:

3 cups rolled oats

½ cup flax seeds

½ cup raw sunflower seeds

ADD INS:

1½ cups rolled oats

¾ cup natural peanut butter (unsalted)

½ cup coconut oil, melted

Place three cups of rolled oats, flax seeds and sunflower seeds in a blender or food processor. Blend until you have a coarse flour (leaving some texture). Remove the flour from the blender and place into a large bowl. Stir in the remaining oats, peanut butter and melted coconut oil. Test the temperature of the melted coconut oil to make sure that it is not too hot, then use your hands to combine all the ingredients. Roll one tablespoon at a time into small balls. Place in a single layer on a cookie sheet, and then place in the freezer to firm up. Once firm, store a small supply in an airtight container in the fridge. The remainder can be stored in the freezer in an airtight container for up to a month.

COCONUT CREAM BALLS

This recipe is incredibly fast and easy and will leave your doggie friends suitably impressed. By storing your cans of coconut milk in the fridge you are ready to make this treat anytime.

MAKES ABOUT 2 DOZEN

1–13-ounce (400 ml) can full fat coconut milk *Chilled*

½ cup natural peanut butter (unsalted)

3 cups rolled oats

Chill the can of coconut milk in the fridge for about four hours so the cream rises to the top. Open the can and remove the coconut cream, carefully leaving the coconut water behind.

In a large bowl mix the coconut cream, peanut butter and rolled oats. Roll one tablespoon at a time into small balls. Place in a single layer in the freezer to firm up. Once firm store a small supply in an air-tight container in the fridge and the remainder can be stored in the the freezer in an air-tight container for up to a month.

WORDS OF GRATITUDE
ACKNOWLEDGMENTS

This book would not exist without the love of my life, Deb Ozarko. Thank you for joyfully taste testing my creations for almost two decades now. I can't count the number of times you reminded me to write down my recipes. Without your persistence, this book would not exist. Your beautiful presence in my life has always been a spark that lit me up, and I am grateful that you were the rocket fuel behind this creation.

A big dose of gratitude to my sister-in-law, Donna Ozarko, who asked me when my cookbook was going to be ready when she visited us in the fall of 2016. That question was the catalyst that rekindled my desire to finally bring this cookbook to life.

Many thanks to my mother, June for showing me how to bake when I was a little girl. I still remember learning how to use measuring cups and spoons to make cakes. Thank goodness there were always two beaters available once the cake mix was prepared so my brother, Patrick and I each had one to lick clean.

Thank you to my sister-in-law, Diana Ozarko, who has always encouraged and believed in me.

Thank you to all the people who I've coached, who have come to cooking classes and workshops, courses and presentations over the years. Thanks for your support, your enthusiasm and your presence. Collectively, you've inspired me to be the best I could possibly be. After too many requests to count, I finally have a cookbook to share with you.

Thanks to Ange, Ethan, Levi, and Judah for allowing me to come and play in your Hawaiian kitchen. Your curiosity for healthy and compassionate food was inspirational for me. I cherish the memory of those sacred days and I am honoured to include Levi's Oahu Energy Bites in this book.

To my friend, Naomi, who upon hearing that I was finally going to publish my cookbook told me that she could not wait to hold it next to her heart. That beautiful image kept me going through all the testing and edits.

Thank you to my beta readers, Sheila Winter-Wallace, Rebekah Nemethy, Linda Marble, and my partner, Deb. I could not have done this without you. I am thrilled to have your essence flowing throughout this book.

And lastly, thanks to Dana Anderson for creating the perfect piece of background art for my cover shot, and to Tanya Petraglia for helping me set it up perfectly.

I would also like to take a moment to acknowledge Chuck Pappas who died in 2011. As a member of the Farm Sanctuary rescue team he was an integral part of the Iowa pig rescue. I spent many hours on the levee working alongside Chuck and was deeply moved by his unyielding dedication to comforting and rescuing the pigs. The unfathomable depth of his compassion was an inspiration for myself and for all.

INDEX

D

E

F

G

P

Q

R

S

T

V

W

Z

ABOUT THE AUTHOR

DEB GLEASON is a former homicide detective turned certified holistic nutritionist and vegan lifestyle coach. Deb knows that cheeseburgers are deadlier than guns. She's chosen to dedicate her life to empowering soulful wellness through compassionate food choices.

Deb offers life-changing programs, products and books that inspire critical thinking, confidence, and vitality. Drawing from her many years of coaching experience, she works with individuals and groups to show how delicious, nourishing, and easy plant-based food choices can be.

Visit her website at debgleason.net and check out her suite of empowering informational products. You'll find courses, classes, cookbooks, and virtual cookbooks with recipes, shopping lists and videos filmed in her own kitchen.

When not creating great recipes, Deb can be found building things with reclaimed wood, or out exploring beautiful natural spaces with her partner and fun-loving canine family.

Made in the USA
San Bernardino, CA
03 April 2018